Faith and Praxis

A Collection of Reflections

Faith and Praxis
A Collection of Reflections

Viju Wilson

2024

Faith and Praxis: *A Collection of Reflections*: Published by the Indian Society for Promoting Christian Knowledge (ISPCK), Post Box 1585, Kashmere Gate, Delhi-110006.

Online order: http://ispck.org.in/book.php

Also available on amazon.in

ISBN: 978-81-19434-61-9

Laser typeset by

ISPCK, Post Box 1585, 1654, Madarsa Road, Kashmere Gate, Delhi-110006 • *Tel:* 23866323

e-mail: mail@ispck.org.in • ella@ispck.org.in
website: www.ispck.org.in

Contents

Preface

Christian faith demands absolute dependence on God and praxis of dogmatic and ethical teachings. Faith (an act of trust and belief system) and praxis (reflection and action) are two sides of the same coin. According to the Christian faith, spirituality does not end with the faith but begins with it and moves forward with praxis. Some Christians are content with affirming their faith in God and an experience of divine intervention in their lives in times of crisis. They find satisfaction in participating in rituals and ceremonies and involving in evangelistic activities. They are reluctant to reflect and act upon what they believe. They also resist to look at the faith from a different perspective. However, others emphasize praxis more than faith. They tend to ignore dogmatic explanations of the faith. At the same time, some attempt to balance both faith and praxis. What is needed is not prioritization but integration: praxis of faith.

Faith should invoke praxis. That is the strength of any belief system. Faith becomes redundant if it does not shape the outlook of believers and persuade them to take ethical positions that resonate with its values. Praxis enriches faith and builds a humane community of faith that exists as an embodiment of faith. It does not happen in a vacuum but through the chemistry of reflection-action. The believers are called to initiate the process of reflection and action. No belief system could remain appealing to the people without the praxis of its followers. They are the locus of faith. Often, the relationship between believers and faith does not reach the level of compatibility because of the lack of praxis. Many perceive praxis only in terms of rituals and ceremonies. In light of incompatible relationships, a question to be asked is who fails whom? Faith fails its believers or vice versa? If we take faith as a living being, it does not fail the believers because it provides them with the content of faith and tells them the ways of praxis. Though they choose the faith for different reasons, the praxis of its content is mandatory. If believers fail to embody the faith, they fail the faith in society. The lack of praxis among believers naturally leads the faith to social and religious 'death.'

Reading the content of faith with 'new eyes' is an important act in the process of integrating faith and praxis. Reflection breaks new pathways of action. The faith becomes relevant if it is read and understood in relation to people's context/life realities. Stories, parables, events, teachings, and biographies (text) that explain the content of faith should be read through the prism of praxis. The relevance of a text/doctrine should be evaluated by its potential to inspire the readers to act. If praxis is the goal, the reader should be allowed to appropriate the text in his/her context. The reader should read it without losing the essence of the text. Apart from the text, the message implied in rituals and ceremonies also should be decoded and proclaimed to conscientize the faith community towards praxis. Perspectival reading/meaning-making gives a framework for contextually relevant actions. The inherent power of the content of faith to stimulate praxis can be released through reading with 'new eyes' informed by people's suffering, struggle, and hope. The faith narratives are narratives pregnant with praxis. Therefore, praxis is an inevitable outcome of the reading of the text. It should not be aborted.

Jesus is the model of faith, reflection, and action. He had strong faith in God, who sent him to this world and acted up on what he believed and taught. Therefore, his life and ministry are the foundation of Christian praxis. His ministerial engagement with people redefined the praxis of faith from 'rite praxis' (observance of rituals) to 'right praxis' (living out the faith with the right actions, decisions, and relationships). The culmination of Jesus' ministry happened on the Cross. The Cross is the ultimate point of praxis where a life was laid down for the sake of life. It gives a framework for the praxis of faith today. His empty tomb provides hope for those who strive to become men and women of praxis. Jesus, the norm and the content of the Christian faith, demands strong faith and bold praxis. He proclaimed the Gospel of Life that offered life in its fullness to the entire creation. Therefore, the followers of Jesus Christ should believe and act upon it.

This book has thirty-two reflections focusing on the life and ministry of Jesus Christ and Christian witness in society today. It attempts to explain the importance of the praxis of faith in community and missional life. All topics in this book locate Jesus Christ as the norm for reflection and action. Each reflection offers ethical directions and theological foundations for practical Christianity. The Christian life is a life of praxis. Reflections in this book are connected by the mandate of translating faith into praxis. Faith gets new meaning, new space, new audience, and new challenges when we reflect on it and act accordingly. This book is a revised version of my articles, sermons, and speeches. Special thanks to my student, Kholou Mekrisuh, for her meticulous reading of the manuscript and suggestions, and to ISPCK and its editorial team for publishing this book. I am also thankful to my wife, Sonia, and children: Sia and Vihaan for their encouragement in my journey of writing.

Dr. Viju Wilson
Union Biblical Seminary
Pune

1

Remembering Jesus
A Call for Committed Involvement in Human Life

Memories evoke different feelings in human life. While some motivate us to courageously face the challenges in life, others make us retreat from them. However, the memory of Jesus through the sacrament of Eucharist (Luke 22:14-23) encourages Christians not to live in a defeatist mindset but with a commitment to participate in the pain of others for enabling them to experience the power of the sacrificial death of Jesus on the cross. How can we make sense of the memory of Jesus in our lives? Is this memory significant to live out our faith in the midst of human brokenness today?

The memory of Jesus' atoning sacrifice on the cross goes beyond the experience of a ritual. Though the Eucharist helps us understand and experience the meaning of his suffering and death, the memory of him becomes meaningful if we deliberately participate in the sufferings of people. The memory of Jesus should lead us into genuine participation. Gradually, it initiates the process of salvific experience in the locations of abandonment, humiliation, and stigmatization. It is also the memory that generates hope in the midst of angst, wretchedness, and defeat. When we remember Jesus, we are becoming 'members' in his life events. In other words, his earthly life calls his followers to participate in the lives of suffering people. In fact, his memory invites us to initiate transformative work within and outside the faith community. It also provokes us to bear the cross of others for their resurrection in life. Today, people do not want our sophisticated doctrines and creeds but participation in their struggles to sustain life. Our faith in Jesus is not an expression of abstract ideology but an experiential affirmation of God who stands with those who suffer. The embodiment of this God is the content of the memory of Jesus. Christian commitment to fellow human beings begins with this memory.

The praxis of the memory of Jesus happens at the place we encounter the hungry, the sick, and the abandoned. This is purely a Eucharistic experience. The God who died on the cross for the wretched human beings loves to see his followers remembering him not only in the ritual of Eucharist but also in the life of Eucharist (communion). It makes them channels of transformation in the world where structures and systems remain uncaring for the millions of people. The memory of Jesus' life draws us closer to those who are victimized by the sins of the dominant. Our one step closer to the struggling community is another step closer to God.

The atoning sacrifice of Jesus has achieved the freedom of humanity from the bondage of sin. Accordingly, the celebration of the Eucharist proclaims freedom through the saving power of Jesus. The people who proclaim and experience freedom in Jesus are already in Eucharistic communion with God. Biblical freedom is a multi-dimensional experience that touches the whole life. The memory of Jesus challenges us to combat against the powers and principalities of this world that keep people under the bondage of sin. Any form of bondage is sinful: spiritual and physical. As a subversive memory, the memory of Jesus has the power to penetrate into the citadel of bondage and destroy its sinful foundations. It implies that Eucharist is an occasion of intensifying the subversive power of the memory of Jesus in personal and community life.

Remembering Jesus is risky because we need to actualize the subversive power of his memory. It involves proclaiming freedom for others too. Proclaiming the gospel of freedom takes the faith community into the lives of the insignificant in Church and society. Unless we engage with them, the memory of Jesus does not go beyond emotions. The freedom that Jesus offered is freedom with commitment. It comes with a commitment to God and fellow human beings. It does not violate the law of God for individual priorities. Jesus is the norm of the expression of biblical freedom. The experience of freedom is intrinsically connected with the memory of Jesus. It reminds us of the scope and limitations of the freedom given by God. The freedom from the bondage of sin is not the freedom for any action that will open the doors of bondage again.

The memory of Jesus gives us a new perspective and vision for the involvement in the issues of people. It calls for the communion with the suffering people as Jesus did. Jesus' perspective of life encourages us to rethink the approach towards others. He looked at the people through the eyes of divine justice and compassion. It brought the people with physical and mental disabilities into his fellowship. For him, fellowship with them was the manifestation of his communion with God. It was also an experience of remembering God, a Eucharistic experience.

The memory of Jesus takes us into Eucharistic fellowship with the poor, the destitute, the aged, the orphan, the disabled, the the victims of pandemics, and so on. One cannot enter into their space without a shift in perspective. The memory of Jesus is the driving force of such perspectival change. The communion that emerges out of the memory of Jesus is for the renewal, transformation, and liberation of human life.

Once I saw a picture of a cross in which it was written: "I asked Jesus 'How much do you love me?' 'This much,' He answered. Then he stretched out his arms and died." Today, millions of people ask the same question to us. What is our response to their question? Can we respond to them as Jesus answered? Remembering Jesus is nothing but a willingness to live and die for others. The memory of Jesus should not bind the faith community only to the dogmas and rituals but enable them to release the power of the memory of Jesus into the lives of people who long for the freedom from the bondage of sin: individual and corporate. When we remember Jesus, we are called to involve in the lives of others.

2

Risking Life for Life's Sake

Leadership is crucial for the development of any community. In the progression of human society from the primitive to the post-modern period, human race has seen a variety of leadership in social, political, and religious realms. When we think of a leader some names or images come to our minds. We often fondly remember a particular leader because s/he exhibited certain qualities that we wish to see in the lives of leaders. Today, we have 'leaders' but not the 'servant leaders' who serve the community at the cost of their lives. Personally, a servant leader is one who risks his/her life for the sake of others in society. Often the quality of 'risking life for the sake of others' is not visible in the present-day leaders of any kind; be it political or religious. The following are a few reflections on servant leadership based on Luke 10:25-37.

In the parable of the Good Samaritan, Jesus answers the question, 'who is my neighbor?' asked by an expert in the law. In response, Jesus narrated an incident that used to happen on the road from Jerusalem to Jericho in the first century. It was a narrow rocky road with sudden turnings. St. Jerome called it 'the Red and Bloody way.' In this parable, we see an unidentified victim of violence and robbery. He was stripped of his clothes, and badly beaten by the robbers. Though Jesus articulated the parable in the context of the Jewish definition of neighbor, it has implications for defining 'servant leadership.'

Three individuals: a Priest, a Levite, and a Samaritan encountered a victim of violence. From a personal point of view, they represent three models of leadership. Their attitude or way of thinking is very much evident in their treatment of the victim. The priest gave importance to the temple rituals and their purity. Therefore, he was hesitant to attend to the victim. In other words, he was not ready to take the risk of getting defiled. For him, the temple was greater than the pain of the wounded person. He considered worship at the temple more valuable than serving the poor victim. He also miserably failed to understand the fact that God in whose name he did all the ritualistic practices would not necessarily be present in the temple. In the leadership models, he symbolizes a leader who is least concerned about the victimized but the systems and the structures that make him/her 'significant.' A servant leader does not overlook the pain of the people but participates in it.

The outlook of the Levite was also not different from the priest. His reluctance to help the victim emerged from the consciousness that he should also not be polluted by the contact of the victim. In today's context, he represents a leader who does not take the risk to go beyond the ideological framework. Like the Levite, s/he restricts his/her space for action within the boundaries of creeds. For him/her, strict observance of what is taught is important than what ought to be done in the context of victimization. S/he is more dogmatic than practical. S/he looks into the ideological position and the identity of the victimized to extend a hand of help. An ideological commitment that does not see the broken life realities of the people is a lifeless action. Jesus very clearly reminds us that life takes precedence over ideology. A servant leader is not bound by the rules and regulations that prevent him/her from serving the people but goes the extra mile to attend to the victims irrespective of creed, color and class.

While the priest and the Levite failed to understand the pain of the victim, a Samaritan, so-called impure person in the sight of Jews, voluntarily puts his life at risk and served the victim. He represents a 'Servant Leader.' He pitied the victim and bandaged his wounds and arranged what was needful. He knew that the road was dangerous, and he could also be robbed if he tried to help the victim. He did not blame the victim for traveling on this road alone. He did not think that the money and energy which he had to spend for this victim would be given back. He also did not do the postmortem of the victim's history whether he was a Jew or Samaritan or Gentile or sinner. Nevertheless, he took the risk to bandage the wounds of the victim. Like the Samaritan, Jesus as a servant leader, in his life-journey met many victims and risked his life for the sake of their lives. Risking one's life does not necessarily mean that s/he has to die for others but spending time and resources with others in their difficult times, avoiding excuses to help others when they require one's presence and coming down from the comfort zones to touch the lives of victims. Jesus did the same in his life-time. He went one step further and died for others on the cross. A Christian leader, who does not understand the pain of others, does not identify with Jesus Christ who always spent time with people, who were victimized for various reasons. The Samaritan, the role model for servant leadership, spent his time, energy, and resources to bring out a person from his wretched condition. The action of the Samaritan reminds us that every Christian ought to be a 'Servant-Leader' who risks his/her life for the sake of saving others' lives in the society. S/he is a symbol of hope in the world of victimization.

3

Spirituality of Solidarity

One of the expressions of biblical spirituality is the practice of certain virtues taught in the Bible. No virtue remains in an idealistic form in Christian faith but demands us to make them realistic in daily life. In fact, they have power to define our destiny. The beauty of biblical virtues is that they are taught by God through His historical interventions and revelations culminated in the life and work of Jesus Christ. Solidarity is one of the most powerful virtues in the Bible. The term, 'solidarity' basically conveys the meaning of "the fact or quality, on the part of communities of being perfectly united or at one in some respect, especially in interests, sympathies or aspirations." It implies a conscious and intentional action of standing with a person or group in achieving a common goal or vision. It is not a neutral exercise, but a political action. It is an act of 'taking side' with those who need our friendship to celebrate life in church and society. For instance, a genuine friendship is one of the manifestations of the spirituality of solidarity. Though it involves risk, it has power to break new grounds for facilitating dignified life. Any act of solidarity makes our spirituality expressive and productive in the locations of 'dry bones.'

The biblical God teaches us the spirituality of solidarity starting from His very act of creation. Though it continued in different forms and levels in the history of creation, Divine Solidarity is best expressed by the liberating interventions of God in the life of individuals and communities. The freedom of the people of Israel from the bondage of Egyptians is a biblical proof of God's expression of solidarity in human history. And the beauty of Divine Solidarity are the locations God had selected in the past. The Bible informs that the life of the broken, disheartened, rejected and oppressed often became the site of God's solidarity. They experienced both social and spiritual deliverance in their lives and became instruments of new spirituality that goes beyond rituals and traditions. It challenges us to reorient our spirituality through solidarity (friendship) with those who live in the periphery of the time.

Jesus Christ, the embodiment of God's solidarity, is the model for the spirituality of solidarity. In him, we witness the praxis of spirituality of solidarity. God's incarnational act in Jesus Christ shows that solidarity is a bold and virtuous action of intentional self-emptying for the sake of others who are longing for salvific experience in this world and the world to come. Indeed, the followers of Jesus Christ are the agents for activating the power of Divine Solidarity with the poor. The nature of God's incarnational act also explains that God of Solidarity prefers to be with those who are in the periphery. In the very act of incarnation, God became an ordinary human being. The people whom God selected to facilitate the process of incarnation were also ordinary human beings: Mary, a poor village girl and Joseph, a carpenter. The birthplace of Jesus also tells us that God wanted not only to become an ordinary human being but also to be born in an ordinary location. The selection of ordinary people, location and living condition for the incarnational act was not accidental but intentional choice. It spells out the purpose of God's incarnation: solidarity with human beings, particularly with the poor and marginalized and become a model for human solidarity.

Jesus' spirituality was a spirituality of solidarity. He actually 'took side' with the prostitutes, the publicans, the sinners, the poor peasants, the blind, the oppressed and empowered them to face the challenges of the day. His commitment to the poor and needy is the best expression of his spirituality. Jesus' life tells us that spirituality of solidarity is prophetic and salvific in nature. Outside the walls of religious and cultural institutions Jesus met the breadless crowds, the broken, the crippled, the exploited working class and the blind: physically and spiritually. His friendship with them facilitated their whole salvation-this worldly and other worldly. When he took side with the outcasts, they were shifted from the margin to the centre. The spirituality of solidarity demands the followers of Jesus Christ to 'take side' with the people who are deprived of opportunities and resources (both material and spiritual) to enjoy everyday life. Any form of solidarity becomes a channel of divine power if it is expressed for the cause of saving those who live a disempowered life. Every Christian is called to live out the spirituality of solidarity taught by God through Jesus Christ. Our friendship with the deprived in society is a bold expression of the spirituality of solidarity. Therefore, the followers of Jesus Christ should reorient their spirituality in light of biblical solidarity and engage with the broken life realities of people.

4

Belief and Behavior

Christianity, like any other religious tradition, endorses certain dogmatic and ethical principles. Ethics derives its authority from the content of faith. At the same time, faith becomes meaningless if the action does not accompany it. The Bible strongly asserts the inseparability of faith and action. It teaches us that belief and behavior are integrally related. They are two sides of the same coin. One validates another. Indeed, the summary of the Christian life lies in these two words: belief and behavior. Who is a Christian? S/he believes in what is recorded in the Bible as the revelation of God ultimately manifested in Jesus Christ and shapes his/her life in line with what s/he believes. S/he ought to manifest the content of the belief system in his/her behavior. The framework and nature of behavior comes from faith.

When I say I am a Christian, I declare two things: what I believe (faith) and how I ought to behave (behavior). I also convey what another person can expect from me. When two things are incompatible in my life, I am no longer a Christian. Christian faith demands a life that is completely tuned by the content of faith. It is both a challenge and a chance. Ideally, a

Christian situates himself/herself in a position of challenging the world where various forms of dehumanization happens. S/he has no option but to confront those forces and trends that do not align with faith and ethics. Any act of challenge reveals its ideological/theological underpinnings. It is also a chance to explain the potential of faith and its empowering nature in the lives of people.

The verbal or written affirmation that 'I am a Christian' alone does not confirm a 'Christian identity.' The interplay of belief and behavior also defines the identity of a person. Though different factors shape his/her identity, for a Christian, identity is formed and expressed through faith and behavior. This is not an ascribed (in reality) but an acquired identity. It cannot be fixed like racial or ethnic identity. Born to Christian parents does not really qualify one to be 'Christian.' Here comes the role of belief and behavior in defining identity. How do we respond (behave) in a particular situation speaks a lot about our faith and identity (personal). In other words, our good work/behavior is the reflection of the internalization of our faith. It extends to every action, decision, and relationship in personal, professional and public space. What comes first, faith or behavior? I would go with Martin Luther who said, "Good works do not make a good man (woman), but a good man (woman) produces good works." A good person is the product of the internalization of the faith that comes through the grace of God. S/he is always conscious of the source of his/her identity and behaves accordingly.

Why do some Christians behave just the opposite of what they believe? Firstly, they are not genuine Christians. They compartmentalize belief and behavior and limit the scope of faith to the rituals. Secondly, they look at faith through the lens of otherworldly life and ignore its praxis in this world. It primarily contradicts the content of the Christian faith. Thirdly, the internal witness of the faith communities also influences the behavior of believers. If there is no social/behavioral auditing (correction or introspection) within the community, then members naturally are accustomed to the prevailing behavioral trends contrary to the faith. Fourthly, they willfully distort the meaning and value of faith. Instead of becoming spiritual beings, they conform to the choices and values of this competitive world. A behavior, which aligns with beliefs, requires boldness and adamant faith in God.

Once, a person who claimed to be a pastor visited a seminary library. He wanted to make a photocopy of an entire book. The librarian denied permission because it violates copyright rules but allowed him to refer the book. He offensively argued with the librarian and staff and left the campus. The next day he posted a comment on his Facebook page contrary to what happened in the library. He claimed that he had a very pathetic experience in the library. His Facebook post took everyone who knew the librarian, by surprise. An informal inquiry proved his post wrong and was intended to malign the institution. Instead of truth, he embraced falsehood to cover up his misbehavior. His action and attitude contradicted the content of the Christian faith he adhered to. A Christian cannot choose either belief or behavior, but a life that reflects the faith through behavior.

We believe in the God of Truth, not Manipulation. Therefore, every manipulative behavior is unchristian. S/he should not fabricate 'truth' and manipulate others' feelings and thoughts. Since we believe in the God of Love, not Hate; every discriminatory behavior is a disgrace to God. We also believe in the God of Promise, not Denial of Promise. It demands us to be faithful to the words of promise. Our faith in God, who is Just, Righteous and Holy needs to be reflected in our lives: private and public. Introspection is required for the following questions. What is our behavior with others in the workplace or ministry fields? What is our attitude towards work? How do we behave when we are in power? How do we behave when we are out of power? What ultimately matters in the salvific process are faith and its reflections in our behavior. Therefore, how do we behave also determines the status of every believer (faithful servant) in eternal life. The doors of the Kingdom of God will be opened by faith and behavior.

The model combination of belief and behavior is powerfully manifested in the life of Jesus Christ. Irrespective of situations and issues, he maintained the chemistry of belief and behavior. His approach, outlook and responses were consistent with what he believed and taught. His actions and decisions were conditioned by the revelation (the content of Christian faith) manifested in him. Jesus' prophetic, pastoral, pedagogical behavior always reflected the revelation of God who is just, righteous and holy. Even in the critical moment of his life, he did not compromise his faith: for example, his request for prayer to his disciples and his command to shun violence at Gethsemane (Mt 26: 36-56, Jn 18: 10). He believed in the power of prayer and asked his disciples to engage in it at the crucial moment in his salvific mission on this earth. When one of his disciples cut one ear of a soldier who came to arrest him, by healing the wounded soldier, Jesus communicated to his disciples that he believed in prayer, not in the sword. Therefore, violence is not the solution. Jesus' life reminds us to live a life that will manifest what we believe.

5

Can Anything Good Come
from Nazareth?
A Key Question for Reshaping the Vision

Once I asked my mentees (Seminary students) to share their visions about ministry. In other words, I asked them what they wanted to achieve in their ministry. They told me that they wanted to become a teacher, pastor, singer, evangelist, etc. After listening to them, I asked "Why can't you go one step further and reshape your vision? Along with your present vision, why don't you think and plan something more productive in your ministry?" What happens is that people have visions that are limited to the situations and the resources available in their hands.

Today, no longer one can say that people from a particular community or region can only excel or suitable in administration, education, research, leadership, etc. S/he cannot escape from taking a new initiative by pointing fingers at his/her hapless situation. Being aware of the exceptional situations, what I mean to say is that s/he cannot simply blame his/her identity or social background and be convinced of the reasons for his/her 'standstill' condition in life. Many fail to understand the fact that individuals are autonomous in thinking and improving. They continue to be content with their present status and reluctant to reshape their visions for upward mobility. The question, Nazareth! Can anything good come from there? in John 1:43-50 has the potential to enliven the hidden talents in them to resist the mindset of impossibility. This question is part of the conversation between Philip and Nathanael about Jesus. When Nathanael heard that Jesus came from Nazareth, he doubted the possibility of 'anything good' from there.

Nazareth was an insignificant city in first-century Palestine. It was inhabited by the people who had 'low social status' in the eyes of fellow citizens. They were poor and marginalized section in Palestinian society. They were despised because of their ignorance of the Law. And they lived in a locale that attracted neither the religious authorities nor the ruling class. The question of Nathanael reflects the social identity of the people of Nazareth. (Leonardo Boff, "A Christology Based on the Nazarene," *Voices* Vol. 30/1(June 2007): 22). In fact, they were the subalterns of the day. They carried the stigma and contempt mounded upon them by the larger society. In other words, they also were the victims of segregated localities. However, the life and ministry of Jesus Christ disproved the negativity implied in the question of Nathanael and gave hope for the disadvantaged.

The dominant still ask the question of Nathanael in different contexts. Today, 'Nazareth' may be symbolized by a village or a segregated locality or ministry location or person/community from where the larger society does not expect anything productive. Is it possible to bring anything good out of one's personal 'Nazareth'? To have an affirmative answer, one needs to reshape the vision in life or in ministry. Reshaping the vision involves certain bold steps.

Dare to Know the Realities

In his essay "What is enlightenment," Immanuel Kant wrote "Dare to know! Have the courage to make use of your own understanding-this is the motto of Enlightenment." The expression 'dare to know' has implications for reshaping the vision. It calls for being courageous to know the realities of our context, church, society, and community. This knowledge supplies materials to reshape our simple visions. The reshaped vision is accompanied by the action that brings forth 'good' in the respective context. The best model that encourages us to know the realities is Jesus of Nazareth. His 'Nazareth' identity did not prevent him from knowing the realities of the people. He dared to know about his society: its structure and inner dynamism. He dared to know how the people were exploited by the ruling class and how the people were made blind to their realities. For me, it might have influenced Jesus to reshape his vision and its praxis. The present generation has the ability, knowledge, and opportunities. They need the courage to know the disturbing realities and reshape the vision for bringing 'good' out of their Nazareth.

Ignite the Minds

Dr. A.P.J. Abdul Kalam, the former president of India, once said, "We need to ignite the minds, thinking is the capital, the enterprise is the way and hard work is the solution." The question is how we ignite the minds. For me, the mind needs to be ignited by the questions. It results in reshaping the vision and initiating the action for producing the good. The questions of Pharisees and Sadducees and the common people and most probably his questions ignited the mind of Jesus to engage with the lived realities of the people. This engagement is the result of reshaped vision. The ignited mind of Jesus led him to touch the untouchable; to have fellowship with the sinners; to allow the prostitute to touch his feet, to accept the invitation of tax collectors. He did everything to prove that something good can come from these people and to change the myopic vision of the dominant political and religious class.

Dare to Dream and Activate

Goethe, the German poet said: "Dare to dream, and begin it! Boldness has genius and magic to it." The knowledge of realities and the ignited mind contribute to reshaping the vision and to generate the power for activating it. Like Jesus, a visionary needs the courage to begin it. S/he may encounter failure or mistake in the initial stage. It is not a pretext for the withdrawal but a context for modification. Jesus envisioned a world of equality and justice (Kingdom of God) and attempted to achieve the goal by taking sides with those who were deprived. He was not discouraged by the verbal attack and the politics of Pharisees and Sadducees. He used every opportunity to help the people experience the Kingdom of God. Therefore, the visionaries should fly in the wings of possibilities. They should not miss any opportunity to activate their vision. Opportunities are the playground to prove the abilities and to begin the vision activated. It also demands discipline, dedication, and determination that Jesus had. The visionaries need to work hard, think creatively, and act boldly to bring something good out of 'Nazareth' situation. Though it contains stigma, the question 'Can anything good come from Nazareth?' has the power to create visionaries today.

6

Experiencing God's Kingdom
in Our Midst

Christian faith is both existential and eschatological. Each of its tenets needs to be understood in the present and future horizons. Kingdom of God is a case in point. Often, we fail to grasp it holistically. While some obstinately advocate its future materialization by ignoring its present potential, others stand for its present realization and ignore the future consummation. Still, many try to bridge the present and the future without compromising its doctrinal substance. In this task, faith gets its praxis in the present and fulfilment in the future. We may know 'what is Kingdom of God', but reluctant to ask 'how do we experience it' in our generation. A Christian is a seed bearer of the Kingdom of God. His/her confessional moment with Jesus Christ is the starting point of partaking in the Kingdom of God. S/he is mandated to channelize its power into the lives of others in society. This experiential and missional dimension of kingdom is narrated in the conversation between Jesus and Pharisees in Luke 17: 20-21. Pharisees asked Jesus, 'when the Kingdom of God would come.' Jesus answered, "The Kingdom of God does not come with observation; nor will they say, 'see here' or 'see there!' For indeed the Kingdom of God is within you." Though 'the Kingdom of God' in this passage refers to the physical presence of Jesus, the expression 'within you' challenges us to activate the faith in Him for the present dawning of the Kingdom, an experience of righteousness, peace and joy (Rom 14:20).

The Kingdom of God found its historical expression in the life and ministry of Jesus Christ. He was the 'Kingdom of God' in person. In him, people experienced divine forgiveness, justice, love and healing. By dwelling among the people, he was enabling them to experience the blessings of God's Kingdom. In his self-emptying life, Jesus followed the principle of life-affirmation over life-negation. In order to mediate God's Kingdom in our midst, we also need to follow the same principle. Only the bold followers identify with Jesus in affirming life against the powers and principalities of this world.

As an experience, the Kingdom of God does not happen in vacuum, but in a context. It gives both challenge and promise. While it takes us to confront the realities that prevent its fruition, it promises a final triumph over the forces of darkness. Every day we come across the signs of victimhood and marginalization in society. The poor, religious minorities, socially oppressed communities, children and women continue to experience different forms of vulnerability. The space for dissent or different voice is shrinking day by day. In reality, we are placed in the location of 'life negation.' According to Gustavo Gutierrez, contextual realities are "signs of the times…they are above all 'a call' to pastoral activity, to commitment, and to service." In my point of view, it is a call to live out God's Kingdom in our midst. It is also a call to stand with those who experience 'life negation.'

The manifestation of God's Kingdom in our midst needs agency. Agency refers to a thing or person that acts to produce a particular result. When Jesus says, 'Kingdom is in your midst or within you or among you,' He proclaims that we are the agents of God's Kingdom in this world. Of course, God is the source of Kingdom, but God participates in history (establishing the Kingdom) through human beings. It is primarily a divine-human partnership (friendship). The Church, "the sign and sacrament of Kingdom of God" (M.M. Thomas), needs to be the primary agent in building up God's Kingdom. The role of the agency is very clearly articulated by Dietrich Bonhoeffer who said, "Church is Church when it exists for others." It calls for practical engagement (personal and communal) with those who are pushed into the valley of pathos. Kingdom in our midst becomes real when we stand for others in the locations of life negation. Becoming an agent of God's Kingdom is risky but empowering and a spiritual experience. It turns sites of life negation into life affirmation. Where life is promoted, there the agency of Kingdom is at work.

The agency must have a perspective. The Kingdom of God demands us to look at the realities through the eyes of Kingdom values. It is a 'look' through the lens of justice, peace, love and righteousness. It questions the life-negating forces and fearlessly says 'no' to the sins of injustice and inequality. The perspective of God's Kingdom takes us to the locations of life negation and motivates us to engage with those who still strive to celebrate life in its fullness. The praxis of Kingdom perspective brings forth empowered and redeemed human lives. This is the sign of the Kingdom in our midst. How do you look at will determine the route of your missional journey: journey through the lives of 'little ones' in society. God's Kingdom will be incomplete without them.

There must be a strategy to build up the Kingdom in our midst. The Kingdom of God cannot be established by money power or muscle power but only by the power of love, reconciliation and justice. Jesus' ministry taught us the strategy: say 'NO' to life-negating forces, systems and ideologies, and actualize the power of love. To carry out the strategy, we may have to swim against the currents in our respective location. Gustavo Gutierrez reminds us that "every liberating initiative is the growth of the kingdom of God." It is a faith-mandate for the Christians to participate in the process of establishing God's Kingdom. Our participation should take the form of new mission ventures that will affirm life in Christ.

7

Beyond Denominationalism

Christian faith demands qualitative life and witness in society. Quality is measured in terms of outlook and action informed by the teachings of Jesus Christ. Today, qualitative faith-life has been compromised in various spheres of social life. One of the areas where Christians in India fail to live up to the calling of Jesus Christ is unity among them (John 17: 20-26). Unfortunately, they continue to remain as 'divided house' vis-à-vis community life, doctrinal position, social involvement, outlook and missional activities. Even some denominations/churches behave like 'caste groups.' They maintain an exclusivist attitude with regard to social (matrimonial) and ministerial relations. They willfully close the doors of dialogue and common witness. Sadly, Christian identity is also replaced by denominational identity. Instead of identifying as 'Christian' we are 'proud' to say that 'I am Pentecostal, Evangelical, Orthodox, Charismatic, Protestant, Catholic, Lutheran, Baptist….' These categories are again qualified by regional, linguistic and ethnic identities. This division contradicts the idea of Christian community as Body of Christ. B.R. Ambedkar articulated the division within Christianity long back in this way, "The Indian

Christian is disjointed – it is a better word than the word disunited-community…Indian Christians like all other Indians are divided by race, by language and by caste…their religion which is their only cement is infected with denominational differences. The result is that the Indian Christians are too disjointed to have a common aim, to have common mind and to put a common endeavour… (*Dr. Babasaheb Ambedkar: Writings and Speeches* Vol 5, 476). One of the main causes of disjointness is denominationalism. No community in India (exemptions are respected) can grow if it does not have 'common aim, mind and endeavour.' We talk about unity (ecumenism), but secretly promote exclusivism even in ecumenical forums. Is it possible to think and act beyond denominationalism?

The need and nature of Christian unity must be understood in the light of contextual realities, particularly the challenges faced by the Christians in society. They continue to experience various forms of victimization, particularly caused by communal polarization and subsequent violence. Though the constitution guarantees religious rights, notably 'the right to profess, practice and propagate the religion' Christians in many states experience its violation by the fringe elements/groups that spew venom of hatred against the minorities and perpetuate unlawful activities against them. The Christians are often attacked in the pretext of religious conversion. In many places, priests and community workers are arrested on the grounds of the false allegations of inducing conversions. Irrespective of denominations, worship places have been vandalized or forcefully closed. The Freedom of Religion Act (different versions) passed in some states is mainly aimed to target Christianity which attracts the people, particularly those who are in the lower strata of society. Christian educational and service institutions face undue administrative interference of the government. They also face the encroachment of their properties by politically influential individuals or groups. Moreover, the social atmosphere is now awfully conditioned by majoritarian religious sentiments. Everything is looked at through the eyes of religion. Even if a voice is raised against injustice or corruption, who raises it matters a lot today. The victims of such an approach are religious minorities, majority of them are socially and economically poor and politically powerless. These realities are the signs of the times which demands commitment and action towards the unity of Christians beyond denominations. The context warns us that disunity, perpetuated by the spirit of denominationalism, must be overcome by the consciousness of one body, one faith and one Lord. Unity is biblical virtue and mandate, and necessary for the witnessing community in India.

The contextual realities locate the unity of Christians within the framework of Christian witness. Life in unity is embodied in every act of following Jesus. A divided faith community questions the unifying power of respective faith. Therefore, as the body of Christ, Christians are called to exhibit unity in faith praxis, particularly in responding to the issues within and outside the faith communities. In the words of Gustavo Gutierrez, "To be a Christian is to accept and to live-in solidarity..." Though it is risky and challenging, this experience breaks the walls of denominationalism and generates the power of unity that brings changes in society. In the context of rigid denominationalism which kills the spirit of Christian community, an attempt can be taken to build up a convergence of Christian denominational communities for common witness (cause) in respective context. It is not a 'doctrinal' or 'structural' convergence but a convergence on common agenda to make Christian community a model for just and humane community. It will help Christians to have collective thinking and initiate life affirming actions beyond denominations to live out the Gospel of Jesus.

This convergence is program centric unity or solidarity than organic unity/solidarity. Denominations are not going to be dissolved into one entity. While maintaining individual identity the denominations can unite on program level and respond to the issues of Christian community and the society at large. A consciousness of one body, though spread in different denominations, can bring Christians together to protect their rights in this land. For instance, Christians should stop presenting the common issues related to the Christian community, such as Christian Personal Law, denial of the equal rights of Dalit Christians, violation of the educational rights of minorities and the question of increasing atrocities on Christians as issues of a denomination or section. They must be treated as issues of whole Christian community. The ruling class, who belong to the majority religion may not even understand denominational differences, may ignore any issue if they come to know that particular issue is raised by one of the denominations among the Christians. A divided bargaining does not produce any result. If there is a united action in presenting the issues of Christian community, it will automatically reflect in the approach of administration. It can at least reduce the negative ramifications of the policies and programs concerning the rights of minorities. While uniting for their concerns, Christians should join hands with other communities or civil societies, and more importantly stand with the victims of caste and religious conflicts. Christian unity is incomplete if they ignore the pain of others. As Jesus expressed his solidarity with the margins of his time, so his followers should unite for the cause of the deprived in society.

The unity of Christians should not be a tool in electoral politics. It must be 'political' in terms of taking side with justice, peace and equality. It should raise voice not only for Christians but also for the common good of all citizens.

The power of denominationalism is such that majority Christians are denominationally conditioned to think, act and behave in relation to fellow Christians. If you identify yourself as a Christian, most probably, someone from the other faith may not ask your denomination. S/he will be satisfied with your Christian identity. However, if the other person happens to be a fellow Christian, s/he will definitely ask your denomination and sometimes, s/he may not continue the interaction if you do not belong to his/her denomination or one that comes to closer to it. Like caste discrimination, denominational discrimination is a fact among Indian Christians. For instance, in India there are theological institutions which claim that they are 'ecumenical.' If there is any vacancy for faculty/staff position, the advertisement for the same appears to be neutral or innocent in terms of denominational membership. However, selection and promotion to the higher positions are defined by where you belong to. Not your Christian identity but denominational identity matters! There are denominations which prefer persons from other faiths to the Christians of other denominations as employees in their institutions or projects. It does not mean that people from the other faiths must not be appointed, but membership in particular denomination becomes an obstacle for many Christians to get opportunities in Christian organizations. One of the root causes of denominational apartheid is institutionalized expression of Christian faith. It demands a believer to be loyal to a particular form of Christianity than the 'faith' itself. It has to be noted that denominational consciousness is more among the clergy than the laity. Perhaps, denominationalism is needed for the survival of structures which bestow the clergy privilege and authority.

Yet, a genuine unity is evident among the believers than the clergy. While clergy level unity is often formal and sometimes a 'stage show' common believers have no problem to worship and work together unless they are 'banned' by the denominational authorities. They know the pain of standing divided, particularly in the locations where they are minority. Still denominationalism is injected into the minds of simple folks. It is often perpetuated with political and economic interests also. For example, if Christians are majority in a particular electoral constituency, the candidate, who belongs to the denomination having less membership, may not win the election. Here, not Christian identity but denomination works!

Is there any way out? It is a matter of fact that denominationalism has already crept into Christian community, and badly damaged the image of Christianity of our time. Therefore, the future of Christianity in India does not lie in the hands of denominations but the Christians who think beyond denominations and uphold the values of Christian faith. While denominations perpetuate sectarianism, faith-praxis beyond denominations makes the Christian faith more meaningful in a context. A witnessing community requires a journey beyond denominations and touches the lives of people in society. Denominations domesticate the faith and block its renewing power. It does not mean that denominations should be dissolved in no time (impossible). But they should be transformed into faith communities which actualize the faith beyond their established boundaries and facilitate the unity of believers. A genuine consciousness of being Christian enables a person to act beyond denomination. Denominational consciousness is practically the same as caste consciousness. Being a Christian means being united with Christ, not denominations. S/he is subjected to none, but to Christ who prayed that his followers 'may all be one.' Therefore, a Christian can think, act and experience faith beyond denomination. The biblical unity is not denominational unity in nature and purpose, but unity of believers in Christ.

8

The Unknown Christ in Poor

It is a common human tendency to extend a hand of help to the poor who struggle in their lives. Often, people are either ignorant about whom they really helped or reluctant to help the poor because the poor are not religious category. For some, helping the poor is not a spiritual activity but only a social action/service. The Bible (Mt 25: 31-46) metaphorically teaches us that the poor are the extended body of Christ, and their realities are the realities of Jesus. It invites conscious interventions of the followers of Jesus in the lives of the poor – spiritual and material. The idea of the Unknown Christ in the Poor is implied in verses 40 & 45 of Mt. 25: 31-46. In v. 40, it is written that "I tell you the truth, whatever you did for one of the least of these brothers (*sic*) of mine, you did for me." Verse 45 says "I tell you the truth, whatever you did not do for one of the least of these, you did not do for me." v. 40 is the negative and shorter counter part of v.45. Jesus identifies himself completely with the interests and needs of the least of his brothers and sisters. There have been different views regarding the meaning of 'brother' in v 40. It is argued that "brother" in v 40 means anybody who is suffering, particularly the poor and the wretched. According to Joachim

Jeremias, "the *brethren* in this passage are not the disciples, but all the afflicted and needy." J. C. Fenton argues that "Matthew probably thought of the brethren here as the disciples of Jesus; but in the original parable it may have referred to anyone who was in distress."

This passage informs us that the Gospels cannot be read without recognizing Jesus' compassion for the materially impoverished, the physically afflicted and the spiritually ignorant. In his bold assertions, Jesus teaches his disciples the necessity of helping the poor who also constitute their world. Jesus also confronts them with the amazing truth that all such help given is given to him, and all such help withheld is withheld from him. It implies two theological truths. Firstly, the physical and spiritual aspects of human life cannot be separated. They are integrally related. Secondly, through the acts of kindness also one can witness to the Kingdom and lead others to respond to the love of the God.

The context of Jesus was one of religious exploitation, societal exclusion and political subjugation. In such repressive situation, He sided with the people who were victimized or marginalized by the structures of religion and the cultural hegemony of Jews. Jesus' approach and attitude towards the religious authorities and oppressive systems were largely shaped by the life realities of the poor. Their life defined the journey of his ministry. In fact, they impacted his destiny, theology and lifestyle. They put imprints upon his ministerial focus – liberation of human life from the bondage of sinful wretchedness. It led him to place human problems above the rituals and the laws of purity and pollution. 'The life realities of commoners' were the driving force behind Jesus' prophetic attack against the powers centers of his time. For the poor, he was rejected and mocked because of his stand on the salvation/liberation of those who dreamed for a better life against the ritual-centered religion and the life-negating systems which were least concerned about the empowerment of the poor in society. In fact, the world of Jesus was the world of the poor. The story of Jesus was the story of the poor. The pain and suffering of Jesus were the pain and suffering of the poor. That Jesus remains unknown to many people in theory and praxis. In our spiritual journey, we should try to meet the Unknown Christ in the Poor.

Unlike other religious teachers, Jesus Christ opted himself for the company of the poor and the marginalized of his day such as the prostitutes, the publicans, the sinners, the poor peasants etc. He theologized (practical-cum-missional assertions) the life of people after realizing what they were (conditions) and who they were (identity). He situated 'human life' as the point of departure while formulating his theological treatises. His commitment to the poor and the needy made his name 'the' perfect practical synonym for the poor. The common people and their wretched life conditions led him to say, "whatever you did for one of the least of these brothers of mine, you did for me." Here Jesus also attacks the false religiosity that makes the people to be confined within the four walls of Church and dogmatic traditions. Jesus' invitation to recognize him in the life of poor demands the faith community to see Jesus through the eyes of the least ones in society. In fact, Jesus was risking his life for the sake of the poor in the world. The gravity of Jesus' words about the poor is evident in the words of Jon Sobrino, "Outside of the poor there is no salvation, there is no church and there is no Christian theology." The Unknown Christ in Poor invites the faith community to place the poor as the subject of theology (interpretation and practice of faith) in whom Christ is present as Unknown. A Christian should try to discover the

Unknown Christ in Poor as Jesus had shown in his ministry among the poor.

The prophetic and life-oriented spirituality of Jesus led him to find his place outside the walls where the untouchables were forced to live and suffer. Outside the walls of religious and cultural institutions, Jesus met the abandoned people, the impoverished, the socially crippled and the physically handicapped men and women, the exploited working class, the people who suffer from poverty, ignorance and disease. He tasted ordinary human life and preferred to enjoy it as if he was sent to be with the people who were in need. This is why he was able to say whatever you did for one of the least of these brothers and sisters of mine; you did for me. The Unknown Christ in Poor values the ordinary human life and attempts to empower it against the capitalist mode of lifestyle. Our journey towards the ultimate salvation should meet the Unknown Christ in Poor to value and taste the beauty of ordinary human life in this world.

Our ministry is to proclaim the salvific/liberative message of Jesus in such a way that Jesus cannot be presented apart from touching the lives of the poor who have less/no access to education, health facilities and basic amenities/rights. The contextual need of the people should be met through the proclamation of the Gospel. The words of Jesus remind us that, whenever/wherever we attempt to help someone who is in need; we really 'help' our Jesus. When we help an unclean person to be clean, we clean the face of Jesus to shine more vibrantly and cheerfully in society. If we cut the nail or wash the clothes of physically/mentally challenged to make them hygienic, we truly cut the nail of Jesus or washing his clothes to make him more attractive in this world. In fact, we make Jesus a touchable and acceptable person for all people through our actions. When we teach a letter to a poor illiterate person, we teach Jesus his\ her language of the person in whom Jesus is embodied. When we wipe out the tears of people, we really wipe out the tears of Jesus. The cry of the poor is the cry of Jesus. This is why Jesus said, "Whatever you did not do for one of the least of these, you did not do for me." Our Jesus is not far away from the poor. He dines with them, sits with them, sleeps with them, and rejoices with them. But a few are aware of his salvific/liberative presence in the life of the poor. Therefore, Jesus continues to be unknown in the life of the poor. Our responsibility is to identify Jesus on the face of those least ones in and around us. We can bring the 'Unknown Christ in Poor' into light only when we hear the cry of the poor and wipe out their tears. This also defines the aim of our spiritual/ministerial journey.

It is very easy to identify Jesus in the Bible and in the sophisticated doctrines and the creeds of the Church but not in the life of the poor. Identifying Jesus in them is a precarious task. It demands self-sacrifice and committed response to the call of Jesus to transform the world. Here the pertinent question is that have we ever identified Christ in poor? Mostly, our humble answer will be No. Moreover, it is not much difficult to draw the picture of Jesus in any form, but it is not that easy to draw a picture of Jesus on the face of the poor. We should be able to draw the picture of Jesus on the face of the people who go to bed without food, the people who struggle to manage their shelter and the people who fight for their identity and dignity. Our drawings should happen in the form of liberative and affirmative action.

It is my conviction that Jesus cannot be confined within the theological formulations, the doctrines and the creeds. He does not want to sit in the throne made by those sophisticated theological treatises, dogmas and creedal statements. He prefers to sit in the broken chairs made of the broken life-realities of the people. Jesus enjoys the simple description of the poor about him than the classy portrayal of Jesus by the intellectuals who do not touch the life of common people. It means, in order to meet the Unknown Christ in Poor, we need to walk a step beyond our traditions, ethos and perceptions.

The Unknown Christ in Poor loudly proclaims that if we exploit or oppress someone, we exploit or oppress Jesus who wants the people to be liberated. When we reject the poor people, we really reject Jesus in the world. It means, in poor, Jesus is still being insulted, persecuted and tortured. Jesus pains when his creation is in pain. He rejoices when his creation rejoices. If we want to see the smiling face of Jesus; look at the unfortunate ones in society. In them, we will see the real face of Jesus in this world. The victimization of the least ones in society means victimization of Jesus. Identification with Jesus means identification with those who suffer for unjust reasons. Christ is intentionally present in the life of the poor. Often, we are reluctant to recognize this reality. The Unknown Christ in Poor calls us to hear the story of the poor who want to enjoy the life in this world and the world to come. This is the crux of the words of Jesus, "whatever you did for one of the least of these brothers of mine, you did for me, whatever you did not do for one of the least of these; you did not do for me." Jesus is Christ because of His identification with the poor also. While He embraces the poor, the poor embodies Him in our midst. The Unknown Christ in Poor is not a theory but praxis and an imitation of Christ in our lives to empower the poor spiritually, emotionally and physically.

9

Persecution and Christians

In India, the religious minorities, particularly the Christians, experience different forms of persecution: direct (physical assault, mob lynching, destroying worship places, prohibiting religious gatherings and conversion, etc. and indirect (administrative delays, discriminatory behavior of the ruling class, religious profiling, etc.) The religious polarization, which spews out the poison of intolerance, results in the persecution of religiously 'other.' Religious persecution is a blatant violation of the freedom of religion. It is neither a spontaneous, emotional outburst nor a product of the conflict of mundane personal or community interests. Rather, it is ideologically motivated and strategically executed. The Hindutva ideology provides ideological sanctioning, and thus determines the content of persecution. In the process of ideologically conditioning the people, it initially identifies the Christians as religious 'outsiders.' In the pretext of 'forced' conversion, the anti-conversion discourses and laws also contribute to the persecution of Christians.

The Christian faith informs us that the persecution can be looked at in two dimensions: human rights and endurance. For me, both constitute the content of the theology of persecution. The former takes us to the 'God of Human Rights' in the Bible and tells us that freedom of religion is a God-given human-right, and persecution challenges it. God affirms every human being's rights and stands with him/her when the rights, including the freedom of religion, are violated. For example, the Book of Exodus portrays how the God of Human Rights restored the rights of the people of Israel, who had gone through the violation of basic human rights, particularly the right to worship their God. The divine intervention and subsequent liberation of the people of Israel underline the fact that freedom of religion is as imperative as any other form of freedom for meaningful human existence. Therefore, in the context of persecution, the Church, the community of Jesus that derives energy from the God of Human Rights, must strive to protect religious freedom.

Faith in the God of Human Rights should lead us to take initiatives of awareness on the violations of religious freedom, express solidarity with the persecuted, initiate legal actions against the violators, participate in the activities of human rights movements, join with similar voices of liberty, etc. Though it is risky, Christian faith demands the community to walk in the perilous path. The protection of human rights is an intrinsic and integral part of the Christian community's life and mission. It gives a theological framework for our involvement in the protection of human rights, particularly the freedom of religion. However, the perspective of endurance takes us to the other dimension of the Christian approach to persecution.

The inseparability of persecution and the Christian life is movingly expressed by John Chrysostom: "This is our life… the apostolic life is purposely designed to suffer abuse, to suffer evils…" In this world, being a Christian is a costly experience and a risky task. Dietrich Bonhoeffer beautifully weaved discipleship and suffering and said, 'discipleship involves suffering. When Christ calls a man (woman), he bids him (her) come and die.' It involves not only sacrificing the personal comforts and aspirations but also experiencing suffering and shame from the hands of those who hate Jesus Christ. For him, there is only one option left for the disciples in such a situation: forgive the sins of others as Jesus did on the cross. The passion of Christ provides energy to forgive the tormentors. Indeed, "suffering is the badge of true discipleship." This suffering is not an ordinary experience. The persecuted shares the fellowship of suffering from Christ on the cross. It gives him/her joy amid suffering. The words of Sr. Meena, a nun raped during religious riot in Kandhamal, Orissa in 2008, expressed the feeling of partaking in the suffering of Jesus, "Looking back, I feel that Jesus is not dead on the cross. He is alive on the Cross and is still suffering." "I feel happy that I got a chance to undergo the experience of being crucified." The experience of direct fellowship with Christ overcomes the pain of persecution.

The history of Christian persecution reveals that the persecuted stood firm in faith and hold on to their bold hope. An example of such hope is evident in the words uttered by Archbishop Oscar Romero of El Salvador just a few days before his assassination, "If they kill me, I will rise again in the Salvadoran people…. A bishop will die, but the Church of God, which is the people, will never perish." It was long proved in the life of early Christians also. John Chrysostom asked, "In what way were the martyrs harmed, whose souls were broken by the most severe tortures? Didn't they all shine most brightly at the very moment they were abused, at the time others set traps for them when they nobly stood firm while suffering the worst agonies?" Even at the point of severe persecution, this faith shines forth in the life of people. Leaving the faith, for them, is unthinkable. Asmita, a wife who could not even see the body of her husband who was a pastor, said "That is the last thing (leaving the faith) I would do in life." For her, nothing on earth can replace his faith experience. It reveals the power of the persecuted faith, a faith that gives hope for the future.

While experiencing the suffering, the persecuted consider their faith as the source of comfort, hope, and courage. They do not immerse themselves in disappointment (I am not negating such experiences altogether) but move on by the energy they received from the faith. The words of Christudas, who lost his wife, reflect it when he says "This earth is not our final or permanent place. We are pilgrims here. That is our faith." Surprisingly, the life of the persecuted is the site of shining faith and the persecution (I am not glorifying it) is the time of being vulnerable but strong and hopeful in faith.

The Bible teaches us that earthly persecution is compensated with heavenly reward (Matthew 5:10-12). The heavenly reward is the assurance and the rationale for the persecuted to rejoice in the time of suffering (Acts 5:41; 2 Cor 4: 17; 1Peter 1: 6-9). Christians affirmed it when they lost their houses, life partners, pastors, livelihoods, and worship places. God suffers (participates in suffering) with His persecuted people (Acts 9: 4). The persecuted are the extended body of Jesus in whom God took human form. Though it is not equal to the vicarious suffering of Jesus on the cross, the suffering of the persecuted has redemptive value. It is suffering that simultaneously manifests the spirit of forgiveness. This forgiveness brings the tormentors closer to Jesus Christ, who is the ultimate embodiment of divine forgiveness. Forgiveness is not a weakness, but the weapon of the strong. It is the forgiving and reconciling nature of the persecuted Christians that made this faith (once the faith of the strong in many contexts) attractive and redemptive for many, particularly those who sought to destroy it. However, divine participation also calls for human solidarity (Christian solidarity) with the persecuted in the time of rejection, humiliation, torture, and death.

The persecution, for Christians, is not the end, but part of the faith journey. While defending the freedom of religion in all possible ways; Christians are taught to face persecution with the hope of redemptive value and heavenly reward.

10

Baptism in the Experience of Jesus

Today's world is a competitive world where no area of life is free from the snare of power-politics. It is played in the name of creed, caste, ethnicity, language, denomination, etc. Leaders of the day prefer to walk in the corridors of power than journeying with the powerless in the 'cracked' and unprotected paths. The culture of power-politics has divided the human community into two – the victims and the sojourners of power-politics. Sadly, Christian faith communities are also severely gripped by the malice of power-politics. It questions the claim of holiness in life and the quality of witness in society. The most dangerous people in Christian community are those who do lip-service on 'holy life.' Behind the pulpit they (both clergy and laity) 'pretend' to be holy with the Gospel of Servanthood. But once they leave the pulpit, they become unholy agents of power-politics. They misuse every opportunity to 'increase' their power and attempt to establish their own kingdoms than serving the powerless. Regrettably, the powerful get warm welcome and undue respect and enjoy the support of believers in faith communities also. In order to get the crump of power, even at the risk of their dignity, some blindly follow the powerful and are always ready to tune themselves according to the whims and fancies of leaders. Wherever the leader goes, they follow him/her and enjoy life under the shadow of leaders. Jesus gives a beautiful response to those who crave for power and position, particularly in the faith community in Mt 20: 20-28.

Mt 20: 20-28 narrates the conversation between Jesus, Salome, James and John. Salome came to Jesus along with two of her sons: James and John and expressed their ambition to sit on his right hand and on the left in his kingdom. Jesus responded to their request by asking a question "Are you able to drink the cup that I am about to drink, and be baptized with the baptism that I am baptized with?" When John and James affirmatively answered the question, Jesus told them that it was the prerogative of his father to decide who would sit on his right hand and on the left. In fact, the request of Salome and her sons annoyed other disciples. Seeing the possible division and struggle for power and position among the disciples, Jesus called all disciples and told them that 'whoever desires to be first among you, let him be your servant.' He taught them a new understanding of power and privilege based on his mission: serving others. He made it clear that he came not to be served but to serve others. The power and status of Jesus manifested in his actions of service. In this episode, he indirectly but strongly laid down the point that being ambitious for power and status in this world is not desirable for a disciple of Jesus Christ. S/he should be baptized with the baptism which Jesus was baptized with. It involves cross, suffering and rejection and powerlessness. The life Jesus lived after baptism gives us new meaning of baptism and reminds us of the need of being baptized in the kingdom values and the suffering of Jesus for saving the life of others (serving others).

Baptism: A Death of the Sinful Ego

The story tells us that John and James were ambitious for the privilege of being so close to Jesus. Though it is not very clear about the motive behind their ambition, it cannot be brushed aside as an innocent feeling. Both brothers might have desired to control the movement of Jesus Christ. In our context it may be interpreted as lobbying for power. Even if their ambition could be considered as natural human desire, it came out of their sinful ego. Their sinful ego evoked the desire to become first among the disciples, which Jesus later corrected them. It is also possible John and James must have felt insecure among the disciples. However, Jesus' response to their sinful-ego is unparalleled in its content and relevance for Christian leaders. Jesus upheld the sinless-ego or liberative-ego that renounces this worldly understanding of power and status and placed 'serving others' as a new criterion for leadership. Jesus' expression 'being baptized with' has to be interpreted in the light of his experience. For me, the baptism which Jesus was baptized with is one that kills the sinful ego. It means the baptismal experience of Jesus was an experience of the death of sinful ego. It led him to the people who were marginalized by the oppressive forces of this world. His sinless/liberative-ego enabled him to understand the people from their point of view. Jesus' involvement in the life-realities of the people is the reflection of his sinless ego that affirms life. It did not inspire him to establish an earthly kingdom but to serve the least ones in society. His baptismal experience did not allow him to walk in the corridors of power. He could have compromised with the Jewish authorities and enjoyed the power and position and became the part of power-politics of the day. But Jesus proved that power and position were not necessary to serve the people.

Jesus' ego was humbleness and servanthood that affirmed life. Practically, his ego manifested in serving others is against the ego of John and James who desired for their own comfort and privileged position. While Jesus' ego stood for affirming the life of others, their ego fed their self-centered agendas and priorities. Jesus' sinless ego motivated him to talk and touch the people who were treated inferior in the unequal society. Many Christian leaders of the day have failed to experience the baptismal experience of Jesus. They emphasize much on formality and protocol when they are called to serve others including their own sheep. Jesus never followed any form of protocol. He was always accessible to the needy and the broken at any time. Once, his disciples tried to stop a leper coming near him because of the existing oppressive social protocol. But Jesus did set aside the protocol and healed the leper. Jesus spent time with the poor whom our leaders often ignore, attempted to touch the people whom our leaders hesitate to give their hands. Why this paradox? The answer lays in the perception and experience. Jesus went through a baptismal experience that destroyed the sinful ego whereas many of us received a baptism of water but not allowing the spirit of Jesus to destroy our sinful ego. We need to internalize the baptismal experience of Jesus that has the power to destroy our sinful ego. John and James are the proto-type of sinful ego that always strategizes for position and power. Jesus is the perfect model of liberative ego that affirms life and questions power mechanisms that dehumanize people. The observance of baptism should produce liberative ego in us. It ultimately contributes to the blossoming of God's kingdom in our midst.

Being Baptized in Kingdom Values

Jesus' life and ministry enlighten us that he baptized himself in the waters of the Kingdom values. He instructed his disciples that anyone wants to become first must be the servant of all. It is the basic principle in the Kingdom of God. For Jesus, servanthood is the primary quality of a leader in his Kingdom. In the episode of John and James, Jesus very clearly distinguished the standard of greatness in two Kingdoms. The standard of greatness in the Kingdom of God is the cross which affirms life. In the kingdom of this world, the standard of greatness is 'power' which controls life. Being baptized in kingdom values, Jesus affirmed the life of others. He advocated the values of justice, peace and freedom against religious hegemony, oppressive societal hierarchy, exploitative economic systems, violent political methods and strategies, dehumanizing cultural ethos and demonic structures. He offered freedom to the captives, peace to the victims of life-negating systems and justice to the victims of unjust orders. Jesus' baptism in the waters of Kingdom values led him to the people who lived in the periphery of society. If John and James had baptized themselves in the waters of Kingdom values, they would not have placed their ambition before Jesus. Today, many of us have been baptized in the values of this world rather than the values of God's Kingdom. In the light of Jesus' life and ministry, we need to re-think the meaning of baptism. It does not mean that we should overlook the ritualistic dimension of baptism. Symbolically, we might have gone through water-baptism in different modes. But its challenging implications in personal and community life are often ignored. The ritual of baptism must be the starting point of actualizing the values of God's kingdom. After his baptism, Jesus entered into the space of broken life realities and tried to empower people in all aspects of their lives. Jesus' baptism was a commitment to God, a commitment to sacrifice his life for others. The commitment to God is inseparable from the commitment to people because God became human being so that they may have life. Commitment to God primarily reflects in various forms of service to fellow human beings. As Jesus baptized himself in the waters of Kingdom values so a Christian (leader or lay person) must be baptized in those values for the sake of others. The experience of being baptized in Kingdom values defines the greatness of a Christian in this world and the world to come.

Being Baptized in the Sufferings of Jesus

In this story, Jesus reminded John and James about the life of the Son of Man. He lived a life full of challenges and sufferings. He publicly declared that the Son of Man came to suffer for the people who were victimized by powers and principalities of this sinful world. He always moved along with the suffered in society. His involvement in the wretched conditions of people points to his experience of being baptized in human suffering. The cross was the culmination of His experience of baptism in suffering. His baptismal experience of suffering enabled him to know the sufferings of people. People don't want our philosophical theologies but invite us to partake in their sufferings. Being baptized in suffering does not mean that we should live without shelter, food and other basic human amenities. It simply means our readiness to be with people when they are in need of divine presence and human companionship. Unfortunately, often we are busy with power politics, and shamelessly engage in the fight for positions in faith communities. Through his suffering Jesus has shown us that true greatness is not manifested in power and honor in society but in serving others through participating in their sufferings. John and James badly failed to understand the mind of Jesus. Today, majority of Christians belong to this category. Instead of knowing Jesus in the way he wants us to know him we try to understand him for our convenience and taste. Every Christian is called to be baptized in liberative-ego, kingdom values and suffering as Jesus did in his journey of God's mission.

11

Christmas: Celebration of Peace

Festivals are an integral part of religious traditions. It is quite common that people celebrate their festivals in grandeur and express their happiness in various ways. Shopping, decorating the houses and worship places, visiting their friends and relatives, exchanging gifts, participating in the religious ceremonies, preparing delicious food etc. are common in festive occasions. More than celebrations, festivals communicate the message of respective religious traditions. In fact, people affirm their faith through festivals. When Christians celebrate the birth of Jesus Christ, they speak to the world that Jesus Christ came to this world as the savior of the entire creation. However, every year Christmas is celebrated in the midst of human anxieties and fears. Often, we celebrate the birth of Jesus without looking into the life realities of people: communal violence, social unrest, caste/race discrimination, poverty etc. The birth narrative of Luke 2: 8-14, particularly 14, tells us that birth of Jesus is truly the birth of the Kingdom of Peace.

The account of Jesus' birth starts with an angelic announcement to the shepherds, "Glory to God in the highest, and on earth peace to men on whom his favor rests." According to the angelic announcement, the birth of Jesus brought peace to this world. Biblically speaking, peace is not merely an absence of war or violence, but an experience of well-being, protection and harmony in society. (Ps 29:11; 86:8–10; Isa 26:3; 32:17; 48:18; 54:10; Jer 16:5; Eze 34:25–31). The story of Jesus' birth underlines the fact that attainment of peace between God and human beings and among human beings is the ultimate aim of Jesus' birth. The peace brought by Jesus' birth is for all people irrespective of religions, cultures and ethnicity. Jesus taught and promoted the value of peace throughout His earthly ministry. Therefore, Christmas cannot be celebrated without experiencing peace in personal and community life. Indeed, the celebration of Christmas is celebration of peace in this world.

Since Jesus was born to establish peace, the celebration of Christmas should be accompanied by the experience of peace among the participants and those who associate with them. Though genuine celebration of Christmas is a challenging endeavor in the 21st century Christians are called to make the birth of Jesus, the Prince of Peace, an event of reconciliation in society. The efforts that Jesus initiated to help people enjoy peace in all aspects of life took him to the cross, the most scandalous symbol of his time. He did not shy away from facing the challenge of the cross for the sake of achieving peace for humanity. He was ready to pay the price in the form of death on the cross because he was destined to establish the Kingdom of Peace where there is no enmity, oppression, exploitation and exclusion. He made his birth and death synonymous with peace because both facilitated the process of bringing peace to the world. Therefore, the celebration of Christmas must remind us to chart a journey with Jesus who lived and died for channelizing eternal peace to the entire creation.

Christmas is not simply a festival. Its beauty cannot be measured by the parameters of celebrating festivals in this world. It is beyond common perception and experience of festival in which people celebrate it for one or two days and forget its joyous spirit for next year. It is, indeed, a way of life. In other words, it must be an everyday experience of the birth of Jesus Christ. It does not mean that God takes human form every day, but the message of Christmas needs to be practically manifested in everyday life-experiences. It implies the experience of peace in the broken life realities of people. Whenever people experience peace, they are celebrating Christmas, the birth of Jesus that brought peace to this world. Thus, we cannot limit the power of Jesus' birth to one particular community also. The challenge before us is how do we make Christmas a daily experience than an occasional celebration. For that, first we need to internalize the message of Christmas in our daily lives. It naturally leads to experience internal peace, which in turn empowers him/her to take bold steps to proclaim and practice peace in respective communities.

The birth of Jesus is for the entire creation. Therefore, everyone deserves to experience the peace promised by Jesus Christ. For many, peace means a liberated and dignified life in society. They long for peace in its fullness: sufficient food, good shelter and adequate medical facilities. For them, the experience of peace is very much connected to the mundane needs that sustain life. Jesus also promised the life that is nourished by peace. The peace that Jesus offered is wholistic in nature. It touches every aspect of life, and every human community.

The birth of Jesus was the starting point of establishing God's Kingdom in our midst. This Kingdom is known for the value and praxis of peace. Therefore, it can also be called the Kingdom of

Peace. In this Kingdom, injustice, inequality and discrimination are denounced and love, freedom and righteousness are affirmed. If Jesus' birth is the starting point of the Kingdom of Peace, Christmas should motivate his followers to contribute to the growth of the Kingdom of Peace. Jesus is not concerned about the worldly celebration of his birth but what his birth gives to this world and how his followers witness to the peace he offered to the humanity. His birth should be celebrated by internalizing, proclaiming and practicing peace in life. By restoring peace to the broken, the sick and the marginalized, Jesus enabled them to celebrate his birth. His ministry invited the victims of sinful structures into the Kingdom of Peace and promised them to bear their burdens and give them eternal peace. In the process of leading people to peace, he encountered the religious and political authorities who paralyzed the life of ordinary people and prevented them from experiencing peace. In his ministry of building up the Kingdom of Peace, Jesus called everyone to become agents of peace and inheritors of his Kingdom.

Jesus' birth reminds us of the birth of a life that was risked for others. Jesus risked himself for empowering others to live peaceful life. To continue the mission started with the birth of Jesus, we need to make Jesus alive in our lives. It demands costly discipleship which requires us to invest our time, energy and resources for saving a person from the bondage of peace negating powers of this world. S/he experiences peace when s/he shakes off the physical and spiritual bondage. This is the moment of Christmas for him/her and the person who risked his/her life in the process of liberation. The very purpose of Jesus' birth is achieved when people are liberated to live a life of peace. The followers of Jesus are called to celebrate his birth by risking their life for others who struggle to experience peace in life.

Christmas gives us the hope that peaceful life is possible in this world if we respond to the birth of Jesus positively. It is a festival of peace because the birth of Jesus brought eternal peace to human community. Christmas is the time to participate in the mission inaugurated by Jesus who taught us to become agents of peace in society. Furthermore, we are called to transform the world by living out the value of peace in chaotic and conflicting situations. Christmas is an experience of being blessed with the peace (physical and spiritual) guaranteed by the birth of Jesus and of becoming partners in the mission of enlarging the boundaries of the Kingdom of Peace. This is not a one-day celebration but a life-long experience. It can be experienced not by the sight of stars and decorated churches but by faith and action alone.

12

Water Turns into Wine…in Life

We live in a context of multiple challenges: social, political, economic, religious and ethnic. As humans aim to improve the quality of life so threats to life appear in different forms. We also witness the collapse of the claim of civilized life in many societies. The social realities tell us that still many strive to live dignified life because they are continuously victimized by the hegemonic forces and exploitative systems. The idea of egalitarianism has lost its strength and passion in the scientifically-technologically advanced societies of 21st century. The self-centeredness has replaced the value of mutuality. The oppressive systems of this world and ideologies control human life and shape human thinking and actions according to their agendas. The social and economic capital defines human relations and social standing in society today. In this context, Jesus' first miracle in the village of Cana (John 2: 1-11) gives hope to the people who long for an empowering presence that will enable them to face the challenges of the day.

John 2: 1-11 describes the first miracle performed by Jesus Christ in the village named Cana in Galilee. It happened in the context of the Jewish marriage celebration to which Jesus and his family were invited. In this story, by turning ordinary water into wine, Jesus responded to the shortage of wine in the midst of celebrations. The place of wine in Jewish marriage feast explains the significance of this miracle. Wine is an important item in the Jewish marriage feast as *payasam* (sweet dish) in a typical Malayalee marriage meal. His presence brought miraculous intervention of God in the life of the host family who would have been humiliated in the village because of the shortage of wine. The presence of Jesus, his mother and his disciples show that this marriage celebration was hosted by the family intimately known to them. It is observed that Christ began to perform the miracles in the remote village of the country than in Jerusalem, the seat of religious authority. He blessed the marriage celebration with his maiden miracle that marked the beginning of his ministry. Though it is an historical event that occurred in time and space, this miracle offers symbolic meaning of divine intervention for the people who live in the periphery to experience 'water turning into wine' in their lives.

Jesus' Presence: Liberating Presence (vv. 2, 8-9)

Hospitality is a sacred duty in the East. If the host fails to honor the guest in terms of food, behavior and housing, it is humiliation for the family of the host. If we look at the miracle performed by Jesus in light of host-guest relationship in the East, by turning the water into wine Jesus saved the family, particularly the bride and bridegroom, from the impending humiliation in society. Jesus realized the shortage of wine and its effect on the ongoing celebrations. Thus, he helped the family though they were not aware of the shortage of wine and what Jesus did at the time of crisis. If Jesus had not performed the miracle there, then the family would have been socially humiliated. The miracle at Cana reveals the truth that the presence of Jesus is liberating presence that sustains people in their disquieting situations. It, in fact, saved the family from the social stigma of not honoring the guests with sufficient wine. It loudly speaks out the nature of Jesus' life and work. The statement of Bishop V.S Azariah aptly describes the liberating nature of Jesus' presence, "Jesus placed himself alongside of those who were weak, frail and lifted them up to a clear vision, stronger presence and nobler life." The presence of Jesus cannot be interpreted within the framework of supernatural miracles alone. Jesus' presence leads everyone into the realm of liberated life that is wholistic in existence. In the context of unequal social life and in light of Jesus' life and ministry, the presence of Jesus means the demonstration of justice, the manifestation of love and the experience of peace both in personal and community life also. The followers of Jesus are the embodiment of Jesus' presence in the world today. They are called to 'turn water into wine' in the lives of people who endure various kinds of humiliation: caste, religion, ethnicity, class, gender etc.

Jesus' Involvement: A Timely Involvement (vv. 3-4)

The story tells that the wine ran out when the marriage feast was at the peak of its celebrations. Now the reputation of the family was at stake. Looking at the impending crisis, Jesus without informing the managers of the party involved in the issue at hand. Why did Jesus do so? For Him, human beings and their problems are the locus of his ministry. It is not restricted by time and space. Jesus could have anticipated the shortage of wine earlier and protected the family from embarrassment. Instead, he involved in opportune time and made his presence liberating experience. This timely involvement not only assures us the presence of God who participates in the lives of common people and their problems but also reminds us of the biblical mandate to involve in the life of others who need the divine touch to stand on their feet. Jesus did not wait to get invitation from the host to perform miracle. He could see the realities in that family. It challenges us to open our eyes to see the broken life realities of people and enable them to experience radical change in the areas where they long for the miracles of 'turning water into wine.' God participates in the stories of human beings through fellow beings. Our timely involvement makes divine involvement a historical reality.

Jesus' Rejection of Ritualism and Legalism (vv. 6-7)

This miracle narrative explains the priority of Jesus: human life over religious rituals and laws. In the first century, Jews strictly followed the purity-pollution laws that defined their social and religious life. A guest was expected to wash his/her hands and legs before entering the house to participate in religious ceremonies or social celebrations. Usually, the water for such a purpose would be kept in stone water-pots at the entrance. However, contrary to the Jewish common sense, Jesus made wine in those stone jars. By doing so, Jesus challenged the Jewish purification laws because wine was usually prepared and kept in customary wine skins. Instead of using the customary wine skins for making wine, he used the stone jars for preparing the best wine. It shows that Jesus placed human problems above rituals and laws of religious tradition. It challenges us to go beyond religious ritualism and legalism and touch the lives of people. It calls for the rejection of rituals and laws that prevent us from knowing and responding to the pain of people. Christians are called to 'turn the water into wine' in the lives of people who are victims of ritualism and religious legalism that restrict their voice, action and thinking.

Obedience to Jesus: A Way to Liberation (v. 7)

The servants in marriage party were obedient to Jesus Christ in the process of divine intervention. They acted according to the instructions of Jesus. They became partners in the miracle performed by Jesus. In fact, their obedience also contributed to the liberating experience of the family in the time of crisis. It means human obedience to the divine is necessary for the experience of liberation because human beings are the facilitators of divine intervention in this world. Obedience to Jesus is not restricted to the experience of religiosity alone. It is a commitment to practice the commandments of Jesus Christ. It heals others' wounds and restores the life that is broken. Obedience to Jesus is costly and risky experience. It requires the internalization of values taught by Jesus to enlarge the boundaries of God's kingdom. It takes the followers of Jesus into the locations where people need the presence of Jesus and help them to witness 'water turns into wine' in their lives.

Jesus' Attack on Power Structures (v. 9)

Jesus performed the miracle in a society where the rich and the powerful were served first in any marriage feast. Naturally, they were the beneficiaries of the best wine prepared by the host at this marriage party also. The social structure allowed the poor to partake in the feast after the turn of the rich among the guests. Often, inferior quality food and wine were served to the poor. The beauty of this story is that though the poor were not the first beneficiaries of the feast, they were the first recipients of the wine prepared by Jesus. It may be assumed that shortage of wine happened after the rich and the socially privileged finished the meal. It is obvious in the expression of the host after tasting the wine prepared by Jesus. If Jesus had prepared the best wine later, then the poor who attended the feast tasted the best wine because they were allowed to eat and drink 'later.' Through this miracle, Jesus symbolically attacked the power structures of Jewish society. It was not the host and the rich who tasted the best but the servants and the poor among the guests. Jesus rejected the priority of social order and showed the preference of divine favour. He used his power to challenge the power structures and led the poor to experience divine favor.

God's Glory in Humble Location (v 11)

Jesus revealed the glory of God against the Jewish notion of divine manifestation in the temple. For Jews, glory of God is always related to Jerusalem temple particularly on the Day of Atonement. Here Jesus without any priest, temple, holy of the holies, revealed the glory of God in a humble home. At Cana, God's glory was revealed in the life of a family who were in difficult situation, particularly impending humiliation. The story beautifully describes God's unexpected visitation in the location of ordinary life. Jesus, throughout his ministry, revealed divine glory in others' life by healing them, caring for them, encouraging them, accepting them and accompanying them. He exercised his inherent power to help others, particularly those who were in desperate condition. In the marriage feast at Cana, Jesus could have remained a mute spectator, but he intentionally responded to the crisis of the family and manifested God's glory in humble location. God's glory will manifest when we positively respond to the crisis of people in society. Our response contributes to the process of turning water into wine in their lives.

13

Crossing the Borders of 'Religion' for Reclaiming Life

Religion plays an important role in all aspects of human life. The ethos and customs of respective religious traditions greatly influence believers and shape their worldviews and religiosity. Directly or indirectly they also compel the believers to look at the realities through the eyes of religious faith. The narrow religious constraints prevent the people from going beyond the boundaries of faith traditions and understanding the pain of others. Though they claim to exist for the liberation of people, often religious traditions either contribute to maintaining the status quo of human life in oppressive conditions or willfully ignore the liberative content of faith. Mahatma Gandhi once said, "It is good to swim in the waters of tradition, but to sink in it is suicide." It is very much true in our present-day religious context where many have become slaves to religion. This slave mentality creates hatred and divisiveness in society and makes people blind to the life realities of others. We dream of a life in heaven without exploring the significance of heavenly life in our generation. All religions have exclusive polemical dimension and inclusive humanitarian dimension. Instead of having a balanced approach, people are inclined to hold on to the exclusive dimension that keeps them away from others who do not follow their path. In the story narrated in Matthew 8:1-4, Jesus went beyond the religious laws and practices to touch the life of a person who was an outcast in society. Today, Jesus encourages his disciples to cross the religious boundaries to touch the life of others, particularly those who live in the periphery.

Healing the leper is one of the first three miracles immediately followed after the Sermon on the Mount. In this story, Jesus touched and healed a leper who came to him with a request of help, 'Lord, if you are willing, you can make me clean.' A cursory glance at the story may not help us understand its wider implications in the life of the faith community. But a careful analysis on the condition of lepers in the Palestinian context of Jesus' time will lead us into the in-depth meaning of Jesus' action in contemporary social location. The life of a leper was awful and distressing during the time of Jesus. Church historian Josephus informs that a leper was treated as a dead person. The condition of a leper in the Old Testament times is well described in Lev 13: 45-46, "The leper who has the disease shall wear torn clothes and let the hair of his head be unkempt. And he shall cover his upper lip and cry 'unclean,' 'unclean.' He shall remain as long as he has the disease; he is unclean, he shall dwell alone in a habitation outside the camp." The Jewish rabbis regarded leprosy as a direct punishment from God for various sins.

The lepers were not allowed to enter the holy city, Jerusalem and other walled towns. According to the Jewish law, there are 61 different contacts, which would defile a Jew. While contact with dead body constitutes first in the list of polluting practices, contact with a leper comes second. If the lepers wanted to attend the synagogue, there were separate chambers with 10 feet high and 6 feet wide. It was also believed that if a leper put his head into a house, that house would become unclean even to the roof beams. It was even prohibited to greet a leper in public places. No one might come nearer to a leper than four cubits that is 72 inches. The Jewish rabbis would not eat anything that was brought from a street where leper had passed by. Some of them even stoned the lepers to keep them away, while others hid themselves. But Jesus, the great rabbi the world has ever seen, violated all laws of purity-pollution and touched the leper who experienced inhuman restrictions in the name of religion. In other words, Jesus crossed the borders of 'religion' for reclaiming a leper's life.

Divine Love: The Base for Crossing the Borders to Reclaim Life

In this miracle narrative, Jesus touched the leper who was considered as religiously impure, physically disease-ridden, and socially outcast. He was denied social and familial fellowships. The painful reality is that on the one hand he was abhorred by others on the grounds of religious laws. On the other hand, his pitiable life situation made him a victim of self-hatred. But Jesus touched the leper out of his love towards human life. It tells the world that the praxis-oriented love of Jesus, the real manifestation of Divine Love, crosses religio-cultural borders. The divine love that was manifested in Jesus Christ reached out everyone irrespective of his/her ethnicity, social standing, economic status and sinful past. He never encountered people on a theoretical level. Rather, he met them in their stigmatized life situations and restored their dignity. When Jesus says, 'I love you' it is unconditional but pragmatic irrespective of the situations in which people are located. Divine love in Jesus inspired him to engage with victims of religious discrimination, societal exclusion and political subjugation. He crossed the borders of religion to touch the untouchable, to love the unlovable and to forgive the unforgivable. The divine love enabled him to understand the pain of the leper. His healing touch and fellowship with the outcasts of society were outward expressions of divine love that was embodied in him. Today, thousands of socially rejected people long for the liberative touch of God to live a dignified life in society. It has physical, social, religious and economic implications. How do we respond to the condition of people who go through different forms of stigmatization as the leper experienced? Christian faith life is based on the Divine Love manifested by Jesus Christ in the life of the leper. Touching a leper, according to Jewish law, would have made Jesus unclean. But for Jesus, the religious laws that did not manifest divine love and unable to understand the pain of suffering people, they should be crossed. Jesus boldly violated the law and healed the leper. Like the Jews of Jesus' time, we are also caught up in the religious/denominational instructions that define our thinking and actions. Unless and until we cross them over to touch and help others reclaim life, we cannot make Jesus relevant in this world. We are called to touch the insignificant folks in society. For that we must internalize the spirituality of Jesus that revealed the praxis of divine love and cross the religious borders to reclaim life. Our genuine engagement with divine love will lead us to cross the boundaries of religion. As Jesus placed divine love as the base to cross the religious restrictions to touch the untouchables, so his followers need to continue their faith journey basing on the divine love that recognizes the so-called lepers (physical, social, religious, economic) who long to experience the healing touch of Jesus Christ.

Human Life: *The Touchstone for Crossing the Religious Borders*
In Palestinian society, lepers would never come near to an orthodox scribe or rabbi because they knew that they would get stoned away. Contrary to the practice, the leper in this story approached Jesus with great confidence. Jesus, who knew the value of human life, did not drive him away. He accepted and helped him to get back to normal life. It shows his willingness to embrace a religiously 'unclean' person and make him clean in the eyes of public. Jesus always brought the needy into the center of his response to the divine love. He came to redeem human life irrespective of its existential nature. Therefore, his priorities and attitudes irritated the interests of the powerful in society. The leper came to Jesus with a mind of humility. He did not demand healing but only said, "If you will, you can cleanse me." He did not share the social standing or privileged position of his family or clan. Jesus responded to his request with a different approach: the leper was not an unclean person but a normal human being in desperate need. Jesus' engagement with his life helped the leper to experience liberation from all kinds of suffering. There was nobody to touch and comfort his wounded body and mind. Jesus, the man for others, encountered the leper with divine love. The touchstone for such bold step taken by Jesus was human life. For Jesus, human life was more important than religious laws. Therefore, he had no hesitation to cross the borders of legalism and ritualism that dehumanized people in his society. The approach and action of Jesus teaches us that nobody is untouchable and unclean. Unfortunately, we differentiate people as untouchable or touchable and from spiritual to unspiritual. What is the touchstone of our mission life? Are we living for God without looking into the realities of 'lepers' in society? The proclamation of Gospel accompanied by liberating initiatives should enable people to experience 'life' in

its entirety. The ministry of Jesus invites his disciples to place the redemption of human life as the criterion for continuing God's mission in this world. It demands them to cross the religious borders 'eternally' fixed by human beings.

The Healing Touch of Jesus: A Touch for Reclaiming Life

The healing touch of Jesus gave the leper a new identity and recognition in his society. After the encounter with Jesus, he was no longer an outcast in the eyes of religious orthodoxy. The touch of Jesus not only bestowed him physical healing but also social and religious healing. Socially, he became a normal human being acceptable (touchable) to his fellow beings. Religiously, he was no longer a victim of past sins, and ritually he became a pure being. The beauty of Jesus' touch is that Jesus enabled him to reclaim his lost dignity and acceptance in society. In fact, the touch of Jesus was the touch for reclaiming human life. Jesus' engagement with the leper explains the mission of Christians today: channelizing the healing touch of Jesus upon the people who live a life of exclusion as the leper in the story experienced. Before we become the agents of Jesus' healing touch, we need to ask a very pertinent question 'Am I a leper?' Physically we may not be lepers, but we are all lepers in the sight of Divine Justice. Though we are all blessed with beautiful and strong physique, our leprosy appears in different forms: greed, passion for money, hypocrisy, pride, arrogance, selfishness, casteism, exploiting others, humiliating others, communal consciousness, blind parochialism, slave mentality etc. Often the priestly dress code may cover our leprosy from the sight of people. The titles such as pastor, reverend, theological teacher, seminarian etc. may also help us to cover our leprosy in faith communities. In the pulpit, we are clean people with impeccable track record in respective ministry. However, we do not realize the fact that before divine justice, we are lepers. Therefore, we need the healing touch of Jesus to reclaim our lives that are stained by different forms of 'leprosy.' The touch of Jesus should transform our inner beings. It ultimately leads us to touch the lives of 'lepers' in this world. The touch of Jesus is available to all who have the humble realization that "I am an unclean person." Our spiritual strength should not be defined by the talent of long prayers loaded with bombastic words or the ability to deliver long sermons or the competence to conduct meaningful services; rather the consciousness that 'I am sinner' who needs the healing touch of Jesus Christ who cleansed an insignificant person to celebrate God-given dignity and freedom.

The healing story of leper asks a missional question: what is our faith response to the people who experience various forms of stigma in society? It also gives us an answer: cross the borders of 'religion' to reclaim their lives as Jesus did.

14

Where is our Neighbor?
A Key Question for Theologizing

We ask different questions in life. While some get answers, others remain as questions. At times, we may not get convincing answers to the questions we ask. For me, every question has 'life.' It derives its 'life' from humans, animals, plants, etc. In other words, we ask questions related to the existence of something/someone in this world or the otherworld. Asking questions is inherent to human beings. God also asks questions! God asked many pertinent questions to human beings in history. God continues to ask questions on human life in society. One of the questions that God asked is narrated in Genesis 4: 9. God asked, 'where is your brother?' to a person named Cain who killed his brother, Abel. According to the story, Cain killed his brother because God honored the offerings of Abel. Cain replied, 'I do not know. Am I my brother's keeper?' God's question and Cain's response in this story have profound meaning in our faith (theological) journey. Though the dialogue between God and Cain gives space for interpreting it from different perspectives, following reflections attempt to understand its significance in the process of developing new contextual God-talks.

A Christian is naturally a theologian because s/he engages in God-talk. Though God-talk may have different goals and expressions, it is ultimately an affirmation of what we believe. Faith always precedes a genuine God-talk (interpretation of faith). Everyone may not academically articulate the God-talk, but express it through simple narrative, testimony and action. Except the experience of faith, norms cannot be fixed for identifying a theologian. For some, s/he must be theologically trained and has produced theological discourses. Often theologizing happens without a concrete dialogue with people for whom we do theologize. A God-talk that does not come out of our participatory experience with the lived realities of people is an 'armchair god-talk.' It may talk about the experiences of the poor or the marginalized but suffers from its failure to know them directly. Though God-talk can be personal (emerges out his/her personal experience), it is the product of one's participation in community (spiritual and social) life. Therefore, theologizing is a community event also. Our God-talk becomes meaningful if it smells the soil (context)! Christian God-talk is both orthodoxy (faith) and orthopraxis (action). It gets contextual validity when it engages with the context. One of the ways of theologizing in context is responding to the lived realities of people.

In the context of broken human realities, where do we start our theological journey (theologizing)? I would suggest our theological pursuit must start by asking the question posed by God to Cain- 'where is your brother?' Today, we should rephrase the question and ask-where is our neighbor? This question will take us into the lives of people who suffer from physical and social challenges of the day. It also helps us understand the missional significance of our faith in the locations of pain, discrimination and victimhood. God-talk should gush out of our participation in the sites of human struggles (personal/

community). The question 'where is our neighbor?' gets multiple answers. S/he may be living in a refugee camp or a shelter or fighting for a piece of land or protesting against injustice or living in a slum or abandoned to the care homes etc. These locations are not his/her 'natural' space but inform us about the stories of his/her wretched conditions. S/he may be a victim of patriarchal and casteist outlook/behavior. The social systems and oppressive forces have pushed him/her into the periphery because s/he has a different identity. S/he is 'other' in color, status, faith, ethnicity etc. Theologizing in this context cannot be speculative but practical and concrete actions. The question, 'where is our neighbor' is both risky and challenging. It challenges us to go to the place where our neighbor fights for his/her survival and dignified life. This is the praxis of Christian God-talk with missional engagement. It involves risky pathways and experiences of divine interventions also. At the core, every Christian God-talk is missional in nature and essence.

The process of contextual God-talk must be a blend of intellectual articulation and praxis of faith. Often God-talk becomes more theoretical than practical involvement in the lives of our neighbors. If we fail to act upon what we articulate about the poor and the marginalized, then we must be guilty of developing a theology for them. They do not understand the grammar of our God-talk if it is not expressed through actions. Instead of asking the question- where is our neighbor whom we have to protect and empower, we use his/her life as data for theological discourses. Unless and until we search for the poor and the discriminated (neighbors) and identify with them, our theological endeavors would be unproductive. They do not ask our theological articulations but invite us to participate in the struggles to celebrate their lives in society. As the question, 'where is our neighbor,' is the starting point of theologizing, so the answer to the question makes up the content of theology. A God-talker should be able to say that 'I know my neighbor,' but not as Cain replied to God, "I don't know. Am I my brother's keeper?' The role model is Jesus, the great theologian, who knew his 'neighbors' and articulated the faith. His actions reflected his God-talk. He lived as 'keeper' of his 'neighbors.' His ministry shows how God-talk leads to life-affirming actions and how they produced God-talk. A God-talk without action is equal to Cain's answer, 'I do not know Abel.' In our context, Abel may be a farmer who is fighting against land acquisition, may be a victim of caste, or may be a victim of patriarchy or a victim of a woman who misused the protective laws. While articulating the experiences of victims in light of faith we should also help them live a dignified life in society. The ultimate purpose of God-talk is to lead people into the experience of wholistic salvation.

If we ask a feminist or Dalit or tribal or liberation theologian about his or her participation in the struggles of people for whom s/he theologizes, for many, the answer would not be affirmative. If we do not ask where our neighbors are and unable to be with them in the time of crisis, we manipulate their conditions in theologizing. Liberation theologians criticize evangelical preachers and theologians for overemphasizing otherworldly life and making believers unconcerned about this world. Interestingly, liberation theologians also talk more about classless/casteless society but often do not take initiative to achieve it. A theologian must be both communicator of ideas/visions and wo/man of actions. God's question to Cain helps us redefine what is theologizing? It is all about breaking the silence and asking questions such as where our neighbor is. God-talk flows from questions in words and actions.

15

Wiping the Feet of Jesus...

Defining a person, particularly a woman, as a sinner through the moral eyes of religion has familial and social ramifications. She experiences different forms of stigma in community life. In the process of societal naming and shaming, she faces verbal and physical humiliation and suffers from low self-esteem. Her presence or friendship invites derogatory comments and feelings of contempt from the so-called 'morally upright' people. The society/religious community restricts her space and privileges. She faces vindictive questions from family, social institutions and religious authorities. Often her explanations do not convince the moral custodians. If she resists, they will assert their authority in the name of tradition, faith and community. Naturally, she goes down in history as a devalued and humiliated soul. However, this is not the story of every woman who was branded as a sinner by patriarchally shaped religious morality. The Bible records a story of a woman (Luke 7: 36-50) who defied societal and religious profiling of her life. She availed the opportunity of encountering Jesus and poured out her painful emotions at his feet and stood justified at the taunt of the self-righteous public. When society defined her as a sinner, Jesus empowered her to start a new journey: 'your sins are forgiven.' Her decision to meet Jesus, indeed, redirected her pathway in life.

In this story, Jesus was invited for dinner in the house of a Pharisee named Simon. In the Jewish religio-cultural context, an invitation to a dinner implied respect and honor. People considered the visit of a rabbi/religious teacher or hosting a dinner for a teacher as an honor to the host also. Simon's family seemed to be a well-to-do family to arrange a banquet. If we look at this dinner from the perspective of the host-guest relationship in the Jewish context, both Jesus and Simon were honored. It also happened in the cultural context that highly respected the hospitality of guests. In the first century Jewish setting, three things would always be done when a guest would enter a house. Firstly, cool water would be poured over the guest's feet to be washed as the guest traveled on the dusty roads. Secondly, the host would give the guest a kiss of peace. Thirdly, either a small piece of the fragrant item would be burned, or a drop of perfume would be placed on the guest's head (maybe oil as narrated in the story). The procedure of welcoming a guest is very much evident in this story when Jesus told Simon that he did not greet him with water, kiss and oil (vv 44-47). The said dinner happened in a typical eastern style of dining. The guests used to recline at the table. It is apparent in the text that Jesus 'reclined at the table.' Usually, the guests would be seated around a very low table so that they could recline on their left arm which would be supported by divans or cushions, leaving their right hand free to take the food. During the meal, the sandals would be taken off.

As the story unfolds one can notice a tension between genuine adoration and formal hospitality. Though as a guest

Jesus deserved all gestures of welcome, Simon did not offer any of them. But he doubted Jesus' awareness about woman's character and questioned her genuineness in wiping Jesus' feet with her hair. According to Jesus, she offered all marks of hospitality out of her adoration to him. Simon did not provide water to wash the feet of Jesus whereas the woman washed the feet of Jesus with her tears and wiped with her hair. There was no kiss of welcome from Simon whereas the woman kissed the feet of Jesus continually. Simon did not put oil whereas the woman poured perfume on his feet. While Simon failed to welcome Jesus formally, this woman without invitation intruded into the sacred space (Jesus' Presence) in Simon's house and invited him to dinner. The unexpected meeting of Jesus and the woman teaches that genuine adoration has the power to channelize divine favor. Formality (ritualism) without the spirit of adoration dishonors both God and human beings.

The woman wiped the feet of Jesus not exactly to fulfill the requirements of formal hospitality. She performed what the host failed to do to Jesus. Technically she was not a host, but she became a 'host' to invite Jesus into her life. She invited Jesus into her life that was wounded by the power of sin and stigmatized in society. Out of genuine love, she wiped the feet of Jesus to affirm her life. In this act, she proclaimed that genuine love was her creed. We also live in the context of religious legalism and formality (ritualism). She teaches that every action (religious or non-religious) should come out of genuine love. One cannot invite Jesus through the doors of formality but adoration.

What does it mean by wiping the feet of Jesus today? We cannot wipe the feet of Jesus physically, but we can follow his footprints. Therefore, wiping the feet of Jesus has to be understood as following the footprints of Jesus in our context. We are called to follow the teachings and legacy of Jesus (footprints). Jesus accepted the woman in her 'sinful' condition. It shows the depth of his love for humanity. He allowed her to touch him and be healed through the power of divine forgiveness. He protected her dignity by rejecting the judgment of Simon the Pharisee and the mainstream Jewish society. He valued her action and counted it as a sign of her genuine adoration. Unfortunately, instead of following the footprints of Jesus we often follow the footprints of our leaders who don't 'necessarily' walk on the path shown by Jesus Christ. In the context of broken lived realities, we need to wipe the feet of Jesus who takes side with the discriminated individuals like the woman in society. Jesus asks us to walk in the paths of peace, justice, freedom and equality. The purpose of wiping the feet of Jesus is to affirm life in its fullness. It has personal and community significance. While encountering Jesus for individual salvation we need to live out the values of the Gospel in the locations of life-negation. Jesus invites his followers to enable others to experience salvation in this world and the world to come. They should uphold freedom (spiritual and social) wherever there is bondage, equality where people are deprived of it, justice where people are denied of it, and peace where conflicts prevail.

The woman in this story is identified as a sinner. But it is not clear what her sin was. Probably, she was a prostitute. Though there was strict punishment (death penalty) for adultery, the Romans did not allow the Jews to implement it but permitted them to administer forty lashes less one. It was likely that society ridiculed her with sarcastic and humiliating comments. She must have been sexually abused by 'pseudo moralists' in society. The attitude of Simon shows her ascribed status in society and his dislike of her presence in the dinner. She appeared before Jesus with an unbound hair. In Jewish society, a woman should not appear with an unbound hair. It was considered an act of immodesty if any woman appeared with an unbound hair. The public used to brand her as an arrogant and uncultured person. In this story, the woman also came with an expensive perfume and poured it over Jesus' feet. The unconventional appearance and action irritated Simon but not Jesus! Whether she appeared customarily did not matter for Jesus. As a sinner, she found a space in the presence of Jesus who did not reject her because of her past sins. As an uninvited guest, she came to Jesus with confidence that, unlike others, he would not mistreat her. She experienced divine love and forgiveness from Jesus contrary to the usual experience of rejection and contempt. For her, the life she reclaimed through the power of divine forgiveness was more precious than the expensive perfume. The risk-taking mentality pushed her into the empowered phase in her life.

Simon represented the spirituality of a self-righteous Pharisee and the woman– the spirituality of accepting her sinful life. Simon judged Jesus for not discerning the sinful past of the woman. Along with the public, he also judged her as a sinner. But the spirituality of woman did not judge anyone but approached Jesus with a mind of repentance and optimism. Self-righteous people always hastily judge others. However, as Simon experienced, they will be unmasked before Jesus who called them white-washed tombs. Today, Simon signifies pseudo-spirituality that covers up sins. He also represents 'judgmental Christianity.' The woman stands for genuine spirituality that accepts sins and mends life. She embodies 'repentant Christianity.' For Simon, Jewish law was imperative; therefore, he judged her within its framework and failed to understand the approach of Jesus who came to give life in its fullness.

This story teaches us that the self-righteous people like Simon cannot wipe the feet of Jesus. It is a risky job for them because they have to follow the footprints of Jesus. In reality, they do not want to do so. Even if they follow the footprints of Jesus, it will be formal, and for reputation and power. They do not invite Jesus for an inner transformation but for finding others' fault or gaining material benefits or social honor. But the woman wiped the feet of Jesus because she needed the touch of Jesus to heal her wounds. It reminds us that the self-righteous people have no place in the Kingdom of Jesus but the 'forgiven' sinners. The words of Karl Barth and Francis of Assisi explain it well. Karl Barth wrote, "*And when once the day comes when I have to appear before my Lord, then I will not come with my deeds, with the volumes of my Dogmatics in the basket upon my back. All angels there would have to laugh. But then I shall not say,* "*I have always meant well; I had good faith. No, then I will only say one thing; Lord be merciful to me a poor sinner.*" Francis of Assisi confessed that "*There is nowhere a more wretched and more miserable sinner than I.*" A Christian cannot be self-righteous but be aware of his/her 'wretched' standing before Jesus who cleanses every 'dirty' soul. This awareness always brings him/her closer to Jesus, who looks at the heart of human beings and transforms the seeker.

Having no consciousness of sin is sinful consciousness. How do we redefine sin in light of this story? Sin is any action that disobeys God and harms any life. In this sense, everyone is a sinner. This is not the end of the story. Jesus can cleanse us every day if we are willing to wipe the feet of Jesus. It is very easy to live like Simon the Pharisee who judged Jesus and the woman than the woman who anointed Jesus. Jesus does not reject anyone who confesses that s/he is a sinner but enables him/her to walk in the path of wholistic salvation. She is a model disciple who realized her 'wretchedness' and wiped the feet of Jesus for deliverance from her sinful past and departure for a new future.

16

Experiencing Jesus' Identity

There was a debate regarding Jesus' identity in Kerala in 2012. The context of the debate was a photo exhibition in which Karl Marx and Friedrich Engels and Jesus Christ were put together in one canvas. The photo exhibition was conducted as part of the State Congress of the Communist Party of India Marxist (CPM). It annoyed both political parties and some sections of Christians in Kerala. While some political voices alleged that the Communist Party of India (Marxist) did hurt the religious feeling of Christians, others found it a strategy to woo Christians into the leftist political front. The debate turned into an ideological battle when Pinarayi Vijayan, then State Secretary of CPM said, Jesus was a *vimochana porali* (revolutionary). Though initially, political parties debated on the issue, it became a clash between the Church and the CPM. Some disagreed with the statement of Pinarayi Vijayan and asserted that they would not allow anyone to question the divinity of Jesus. Others supported the statement of Vijayan and observed that Jesus might not be a *vimochana porali* for those who exploit the people through educational-charitable-health institutions established in the name of Jesus. They were referring to the institutional and political clout of the Church in Kerala. These views were reflected in the statements of Mr. Ommen Chandy, a member of the Indian Orthodox Church and then Chief Minister and P.J. Joseph, a Roman Catholic and then Kerala Irrigation Minister. While the former condemned the entire debate and commented that 'it is blasphemy,' the latter said, 'it is a welcome to see that Jesus is portrayed as a revolutionary.'

This discussion gives scope for reflecting on the identity of Jesus. The question, 'who do you say I am?' in Matthew 16:13-20, opens horizons for understanding the identity of Jesus from different dimensions. This question and the debate mentioned earlier revolve around the identity of Jesus. Identity answers 'who am I?' Identity gets formed through different factors. It is an outcome of the interface of multiple components. Though an individual can decide how s/he should assert his/her identity, s/he carries multiple identities. S/he cannot fix himself/herself within the frame of one identity marker. Even if s/he wants to do so, it may not happen in societal life. Human beings may prefer one identity to another but s/he cannot get out of the web of multiple identities shaped by social, religious, linguistic, cultural, geographical experiences. In fact, identity is a 'plural' reality. At the same time, every identity is a 'construct.' Humans construct identities in respective contexts. In that process, some are claimed; others are ascribed. In the Indian context, caste and religion play a major role in the construction of identities.

Jesus asked his disciples, 'who do people say the Son of Man is?' They said, 'some say John the Baptist; others say Elijah; and still others, Jeremiah or one of the prophets.' Then he asked again 'who do you say I am?' Then Simon Peter answered, 'You are the Christ, Son of Living God." Peter's answer and Jesus' acknowledgment showed that Peter revealed the identity which

Jesus wanted to reveal to his disciples. However, he also did not reject what people said about him. Though Jesus was aware of his 'Christ' identity, he had no hesitation to identify with other 'lived' identities in his society.

Identify with Identities

Jesus started the dialogue with his disciples by asking a question of identity. Jesus knew that he was Christ. Instead of proclaiming it publicly, he wanted to know it from others. Perhaps, Jesus asked the question to Peter because of two reasons. Firstly, people attributed different identities to him. It is implied in v. 14. Secondly, he wanted to make sure that at least his disciples must know his identity. It is obvious in v. 15. Jesus wanted to assert his identity in the context of multiple identities ascribed by the people. He used a different method – asserting the identity through Peter. It implies that every identity is relational. It gets approved and known through social relations. Jesus' identity as Christ is affirmed by Peter who witnessed the life and ministry of Jesus. The dialogue between Jesus and Peter teaches that discerning and recognizing the identity of a person or community is a biblical act. It requires us to accept and value the identity of others. Every identity is unique whether it is inferior or superior in light of social structures and ideologies. Peter declared Jesus' identity out of his experience with Jesus. It might be a divine revelation as Jesus said, but his encounter, interaction, fellowship, companionship with Jesus cannot be overlooked. At the same time, Jesus is Christ not because of Peter's affirmation but primarily because of his divine essence and mission. However, Peter's act of confession takes us into the praxis dimension of identity assertion. There are millions who long to get their identities valued and recognized in society. They want others to acknowledge their lived identities. The dominant identities tell them that they carry inferior status in the hierarchy of social structures. Recognizing identity is equal to protecting the life that embodies it. If we value the identity of a person, then we naturally love, respect and identify with him/her. If we devalue his/her identity, we tend to marginalize and dehumanize him/her. Jesus accepted the identity of everyone-Leper, Samaritan, Gentile, Roman, Syrophoenician etc. He took sides with them when the dominant identities (religious, social and political) devalued them. He enjoyed the beauty of different identities. He even learned from them and taught through them. His engagement with different identities demands his followers to identify with identities, particularly marginalized identities.

Jesus' Identity: A Revolutionized Identity

In the above-mentioned debate, Jesus was identified as a revolutionary. This revolutionary identity of Jesus was 'constructed' within the ideological framework of Marx and Engels. We may disagree with defining Jesus as revolutionary. In fact, he was revolutionary! However, he was not as revolutionary as Marxist ideologues understand today in terms of class struggle. He was revolutionary not because he believed in societal change through violence. He never encouraged physical violence nor involved in violent activities except his angry behavior at the Jerusalem temple. He was revolutionary in the sense that he revolutionized human thinking, religious outlook and social relations in his society. His revolutionary engagement was pro-life and prophetic in nature. He was revolutionary in lifestyle, words and deeds. He advocated something new: new thoughts, new ideas, new way of life, new culture and new worldview. For example, he did not demand or command the people to touch the leper, but he touched. It revolutionized the attitude of people towards lepers. It was his touch that symbolized his revolutionary life, not the healing per se. He was a revolutionary because of his life, the life for others; because of his mission, the liberative mission and because of his vision, the Kingdom of God. He was not a revolutionary who attempted a peripheral change but an internal and lasting change in all aspects of life. This change is not to be achieved by physical force but by divine power. It is a change of mind, a voluntary change. In biblical language, we call it repentance. Jesus was revolutionary who attempted to bring the inner transformation (biblically speaking salvation) which leads to community transformation. It is a wholistic experience.

Experiencing the Identity

Some want to monopolize Jesus in their thinking. They have the wrong notion that what they say about Jesus is right. Jesus is beyond our thinking and interpretations. We cannot limit Jesus to a particular ideology or theological system. Then what can we do? Our Christological affirmations become meaningful when we apply Jesus' identity in our lives. It is easy to say that Jesus is our Savior. While affirming the faith we need to ask, how does the Savior work through us? How do we revolutionize our lives in tune with the life of our Savior? If we say Jesus is revolutionary, the revolutionized life of Jesus should reflect in us.

To understand and apply the identity of Jesus we should become spiritual believers than dogmatic believers. Dogmatic believers prioritize dogma, rites, structures, traditions. For them, what dogma says about Jesus is right and eternal truth. Christians, who object to the interpretations of non-believers, do not necessarily try to follow what Jesus said. They do not accept anything outside of their dogma. This approach does not help them own Jesus. Therefore, Christians should become spiritual believers. They do not get offended when they hear anything contradictory to their Christology. They patiently listen and examine the facts. They give priority to the scripture and try to live out what they believe.

What we say about Jesus does not matter much, but how we experience what we say about him does matter. Out of his experience, Peter said that 'Jesus is Christ.' If we affirm Jesus as Savior, we should experience that Savior in all aspects of our lives. Instead of monopolizing 'Christology' we should experience the identity of Jesus. Out of his reading, Pinarayi Vijayan said that Jesus was a revolutionary. But Christians, based on their experience with Jesus, should demonstrate that Jesus is more than a revolutionary if the ascribed identity limits the real picture of Jesus.

17

Spirituality in the Age of Technology

All religious traditions talk about spirituality. Though it is difficult to have a unanimous view on spirituality, it can be said that "Spirituality concerns the way our meditations, contemplations, prayers, and whatever we do in terms of our religiosity influencing our conduct, our behavior, our way of life, our view of life, our manner of life, our attitude to other people and so on." (Samson Prabhakar, *Reflections on Spirituality*, Bangalore: The Author, 2006, 4). Some may understand spirituality as an expression of observing certain religious rituals/practices and of preparing life for 'heaven' completely dissociated with this world. For others, a spiritual person means one who lives a life according to the percepts of respective religious traditions. It refers to the internalization of theological and ethical values. Christian spirituality based on the teachings of Jesus Christ teaches that spiritual life is not a life that is completely independent of this world, rather a life that lives out the faith in context. It is a way of life. It is also a quest for the praxis of faith that culminates in eschatology. Therefore, faith and action are equally important in Christian spirituality. While rituals/religious observances are important for developing a spiritual life, an authentic spiritual life is marked by the praxis of faith in social life. It is a life to be lived in the Spirit and to be guided by the Spirit. Jesus is the role model of authentic spiritual life. He was led by the Spirit in every stage of his life. He revealed an authentic human life which was actually a spiritual life. An authentic human being is a spiritual being too.

We live in a technologically advanced world. Technology has been playing both empowering and destructive roles in human history. The printing press, telephone, internet, medical equipment etc. continue to enable human beings to progress in life. It also tempts them to produce highly sophisticated and deadly weapons and use them against fellow beings. Its destructive role plays out well through the production and marketing of weapons. In this process, human beings are solely responsible for it! Today, no area of human life is untouched by the rays of technology. The use of technologies also raises a lot of questions – ethical, social, economic, spiritual. We have come to an age where technologies (values of technology) define human life than religio-cultural values. The possession of technologies determines the status of a country, whether it is a global power or local power in the competitive world. Even an individual's social standing depends on his/her exposure to the benefits of technologies in society. We also witness the debate on whether technology improves the human condition or worsens it. While the advocates of technology strongly argue that human progress primarily depends on the use of technology, environmentalists and others dispute the claim and say that it harms the environment and promotes individualism. There is truth in both positions depending on the use or misuse of technologies.

In this debate, questions also may be raised whether technology (use or misuse) has affected or modified, or improved our spirituality? Does technology help to build up a Biblical Faith Community? It is a proven fact that technology is never concerned about how much harm it does to humanity, but how much does it help Corporates to amass wealth and manipulate power. It has already conditioned the human mind to think about life within the framework of tools/machinery than through the lens of spirituality. It has altered the nature of human relations and even religious life. If we do not 'worship' technology, we are outdated or primitive. In such context, I would like to highlight some biblical insights which may help us reaffirm our spirituality in the age of technology.

Not by Faith in Technology but by Faith in God (1 Sam.17:38-50)
According to the story narrated in the Bible (I Sam 17: 38-50), there was a good preparation for the battle between Jews and Philistines represented by David and Goliath. David was not comfortable with the tunic and armaments of Saul. Goliath came with the well-sophisticated weaponry of his time. In other words, he put faith in technology and came to the battlefield. David came against the Philistine in the name of the Lord Almighty and claimed that battle belonged to the Lord. Goliath symbolized the power of technology, whereas David the power of faith in God who is not limited by technology. They also represented two spiritualities: one is guided by faith in God and the other by faith in technology and human power.

We live in a context where technology appears as the source of solutions to human problems. The over-dependency in and the indiscriminate use of technology contribute to individualism and technologically categorize human beings as 'haves' and 'have-nots.' It keeps the people within the four walls of homes and makes them selfish and competitive. It cuts down fellowship and relationships. As a result, technology-sponsored unequal and disconnected individuals and societies emerge in the world. Today, we are already 'Facebook/WhatsApp communities' rather than 'face to face communities' as God wants us to be. Technology also manufactures a notion that if you live in the web of technologies, you are civilized and advanced. You are primitive if you fail to run with technological advancements. Many people keep their faith in technology as if it determines their destiny. They fail to maintain the same amount of faith in God, and often technology replaces God in their behavior and attitude towards life. They believe in the promise and reliability of technology than God who is the source of wisdom behind all technologies. God did not introduce any technology that intends to destroy humanity and manipulate the creation. Technology tends to release enormous energy that has the potential to disturb human life. But faith in God reminds us not to be carried away by the temptations of technology.

Faith in technology works with the mindset of short-cuts and easygoing. Technology does not think of moral restraints but facilitates the accumulation of money, wealth, power etc. It provides tools to dominate the universe and gives signals to go ahead without seeing the plight of people. Technology never regrets or apologizes for its sins against humanity but justifies them by its benefits. Faith in technology cannot build up a community that walks an extra mile to see the pain of others. But spirituality built upon the foundation of genuine faith in God can transform the world faster than technology does. We need to develop a spirituality that is guided by absolute faith in God, the only solution than the faith in technology which demands us to compromise the faith and its values in life.

Not by the Money Power but by the Power of Gospel *(Mk. 10:17-31)*

The Gospel of Mark narrates the conversation between Jesus and a rich young man. He asked Jesus, 'What must I do to inherit eternal life?' After hearing Jesus' answer, the young wealthy man became sad and left. He became gloomy because Jesus touched the area that the young man considered so important. Today, in metropolitan cities, most of the educated youngsters work in the fields of technology. It gives them wealth, power and resources for luxurious life.

The driving force behind today's technological advancement are monetary benefits than community building. The multinational companies either buy the patent of a particular technology or invest money in new inventions. Their main agenda is to get maximum profit at the cost of common people. Once they get back their capital, they may make particular technology accessible to all at affordable prices. It means they not only exploit the rich but also the poor. Technology rests on money power and pushes the people to enjoy its possibilities at any cost. The new trends in life compel people to run behind and depend on technology excessively. The truth of the matter is that often we forget the core value of faith in the midst of technological currents. We tempt to uphold the value of technology than the value of the Gospel in social/community life. The Gospel does not promote the power of money but releases the power of love that destroys different walls of separation (social, racial economic etc.) Technology makes us proud and disconnected communities/individuals (creating different walls of separation) whereas the Gospel makes us a humble and connected community.

Technology has already conditioned our minds to be more concerned about being connected to 4G or 5G, for example, than being connected through the Gospel. When telecom companies say they can change life, we blindly believe it. But many of us are not passionate to experience and say that the Gospel can change lives too. It explains our spirituality! While money motivates us to go behind technology, the Gospel inspires us to go behind the power of God. Technology does not build a community of love, equality, justice and righteousness. To develop such a community, we need to nurture a spirituality informed by the praxis of the Gospel. Human beings are saved not by the power of technology, one of the sources of money, but by the power of '*Logos* became flesh.'

Not by the Confidence in Flesh but by the Confidence in God (Phil. 3: 1-11)

Technology persuades human beings to place their confidence in the power and possibilities of machinery. For instance, in the hospital, we tend to depend on doctors than God because they have access to medical technology. It leaves behind God and proclaims that 'technology is god.' In other words, God has been made a 'mute spectator' in the world of technology. But God smiles and says that confidence in technology is just like confidence in the flesh which is perishable and fragile. Technology may help human beings meet some of their needs and overcome certain challenges in this world. The ultimate solution to his/her existential crisis comes from God. Trusting in God helps humans to sail through every form of crisis. Technology does not satisfy the insatiable human mind but introduces new 'want' every day and puts him/her in mental and physical vulnerability.

The confidence in technology and confidence in God point to two kinds of spirituality. The spirituality of technology envisions a world in which the powerful become more powerful whereas the biblical spirituality (spirituality characterized by the confidence in God) envisions Kingdom of God where the powerless becomes powerful. The spirituality of technology promotes wisdom of the powerful whereas the biblical spirituality upholds wisdom of the weak who seeks peace and justice. The spirituality of technology creates club of nuclear powers whereas the biblical spirituality builds up community of peace-makers. Many have started singing Psalm 23 in their lives in this way, "Technology is my shepherd, I shall not want. It leads me to the green pastures of Facebook and Twitter and the waters of Webpages etc...." Therefore, technology should not decide our morality and faith. We should become the electrode of spirituality that is shaped by the values of Gospel. It is a paradox that we do not forget to update the software but fail to update our spirituality. In the age of technology, biblical spirituality reminds us that technology should not be allowed to replace God in human life.

18

Speaking the Truth in Love

Christians believe in Jesus Christ who proclaimed that "I am the Truth" (Jn 14:6). Christian faith, based on this affirmation, requires Christians to speak the truth. The motto of some of the Christian institutions also reflects the biblical imperative of speaking the truth. For instance, 'Speaking the Truth in Love' is the motto of Union Biblical Seminary, Pune. Indian Christians are citizens of a nation whose national emblem carries the expression, *satyameva jayate* (Truth Alone Triumphs) taken from *Mundaka Upanishad.* This nation also has produced many social reformers who boldly spoke and exposed the truth in the social, religious, and political realms of life. Jyotirao Phule started "Truth Seeking Society" to fight against caste oppression and religious hegemony of Brahmins in society. Though religions, ideologies, philosophies and different knowledge systems claim to uphold 'truth' unfortunately our society at large witnesses the attempts of suppressing the truth. Those who speak the truth are persecuted, silenced, sidelined or brutally killed. Many stand for convenient versions of truth in social and religious life. In India, many Right to Information (RTI) activists and journalists lost their lives because they attempted to bring out the truth. Li Wenliang, the doctor who warned of the spread of the Coronavirus, was threatened and silenced in China. These instances speak about the cost of speaking the truth in this world.

We live in the context that endorses half-truths or convenient versions of truth and attempts to suppress the truth. Paul, in his *Epistle to the Ephesians*, particularly chapter 4, encourages the believers in Ephesus to speak the truth in love. In chapter 4, he starts his exhortations with advice 'to live a life worthy of the calling.' Later he talks about the need for unity in the body of Christ. Then he warns them that they are no longer infants who should be tossed back and forth by the teaching and by the cunning and craftiness of people who are deceitful schemers (vv 14-16). But speak the truth in love! In other words, in the midst of half truths or convenient versions of the truth, speak the truth so that you may grow up into Christ, the Truth. It means spiritual growth (growing intimate communion with Christ) depends on the attitude of believers in upholding the truth: doctrinal or non-doctrinal (work, ministry, administration, leadership, family, interpersonal relations etc.).

Speaking the Truth in Love: Sign of Spiritual Maturity (v 15)

The destiny of every Christian is to 'grow up into him' (v 15). It refers to the condition of Christ-likeness in believers. I understand it as a journey of spiritual maturity. Speaking the truth in love is an essential ingredient in the process of 'growing up into him.' In other words, it is a sign of spiritual maturity. This is an experiential sign to be manifested in the life of a person who follows Jesus Christ, the embodiment of Truth. In his earthly life, Jesus spoke the truth in love. He encountered the rulers and religious authorities by speaking the truth in love. He spoke the truth about justice in the context of injustice, taught and practiced the truth about love to the unlovable and the unloved.

He had no hesitation to call those who suppressed the truth or pretended to be ignorant of truth as white-washed tombs or brood of vipers. In fact, Jesus' crucifixion was the culmination of his mission of revealing the truth to the world. To grow up unto him, we need to speak the truth. Every Christian has the mandate to be matured in Christ. A matured Christian cannot hide the truth but stands for the truth and lives out the truth even at the cost of his/her life. S/he is a synonym of truth or embodiment of truth in society. S/he says 'no' to the words of falsehood and manipulation. S/he does not stand with a person or for an ideology that suppresses the truth. S/he does not manipulate people or documents/records but makes the truth shine forth in the public domain. S/he is aware that s/he cannot manipulate God to suppress the truth.

A person, family, organization, church, or an institution cannot carry the identity of Christian, if s/he/it does not walk in the footprints of truth taught by Jesus. The space for expressing the truth must be wider in a Christian family, workplace and community. Speaking the truth is a risky task but Christians have no other option because they are mandated to be matured in Christ. It happened in the life of Jesus, the Apostles and the early Christian Community. Christians need to demonstrate the boldness to speak the truth irrespective of consequences. In the name of love, friendship, community or help extended, Christians cannot take side with falsehood. Not speaking the truth is 'sin.'

***Truth Speaking Community* (Community of Truth Speakers): *Result of the Risk of Speaking the Truth in Love* (v. 16)**
Though speaking the truth is risky it does not go without a result. The birth of truth speaking community is the outcome of the risk taken for speaking the truth. Speaking the truth is

like a birth pang experienced by a mother. Christians had the identity of Truth Speakers. Today, some remnants who speak the truth live among them. They give us hope that Christians can restore their 'lost' identity. Jesus inaugurated the truth-speaking community in his earthly ministry. We need to facilitate its growth. It grows in love because it speaks the truth. In building up this community, everyone has a role: to speak the truth but in love. There is a common goal (building up the community of truth speakers) and a common role (speak the truth). If Christians think of their chairs, offices, positions, and privileges at the time of the need of speaking the truth, Truth Speaking Community does not emerge. With humility and an introspective mind, Christians should ask 'Am I a truth speaker?' 'Is my family a family of truth speakers?' 'Is my Church a Truth Speaking Community?' One may easily claim that 'I am a Truth Speaker' in terms of speaking the truth about God, Jesus, Salvation (doctrinal proclamations). S/he may not be able to genuinely claim the praxis of proclaimed truth in his/her life. Truth should be spoken and practiced. A truth speaker cannot stand with manipulators, schemers, avengers, and rumor mongers. A faith community is truly a faith community when it exists for and speaks the truth. The statement of Martin Luther King Jr summarizes the importance of speaking the truth, "There comes a time when silence is betrayal." Silence is neither a virtue of wise wo/men nor a sign of maturity in a time that demands to speak the truth. If Christians do not speak the truth, that is a betrayal of truth, their faith and morality.

19

'Back to Church' in the Post-Pandemic Context

The Covid 19 pandemic has altered the nature of the Church, particularly the form of conducting worship globally. It has challenged the Church with a problem and a possibility. While it restricted physical fellowship and worship for many months, it also opened new avenues for gathering. It has taken Church-life online and compelled believers to adjust to the 'new normal.' However, communication technology has opened new windows and kept Church life 'alive' in the context of lockdown and social/physical distancing. Unfortunately, we had to say 'yes' to social distancing that is not theologically compatible with the Christian understanding of worship. Though there was discomfort among believers to adjust to the online 'Church life' in the initial stage, they embraced it as they could not find out another alternative. While some interpreted it as a gift of God and participated in online church life, others engaged in it with hesitation. Nevertheless, the new trend of online worship and other fellowships continues to influence many believers even after offline Church life has started. Sadly, many have questioned the need for physical church/offline fellowship without understanding the significance of the Church in the life of a believer. They ask why don't we continue with online Church life? Along with post-modern thinking, Covid 19 pandemic has intensified the individualistic approach that pushes many believers into thinking of Christian life without an offline Church. The danger of this approach is a gradual decline of the nature and purpose of the Church among the believers. Many love to continue online because it does not demand physical presence through which 'Church' becomes a space for spiritual and physical koinonia, kerygma, hospitality, caring for the poor, sharing the resources etc. Online is not an alternative to offline Church life. Back to physical Church is the need of the hour because our faith demands so.

Christian faith is a communitarian faith that requires its adherents to express it inwardly and outwardly. While individual commitment to faith is mandatory, it manifests in community life. The doctrinal and ethical teachings of Christian faith have communitarian value even though an individual is the point of departure. An individual begins to shape his/her faith by engaging with different layers of community faith-life. Co-believers contribute to nurturing his/her spirituality. The mutual enrichment enables the believers to activate their faith in different spheres of socio-religious life. This communitarian faith-life is normative for Christians. The Church is one of the means through which believers affirm individual and community praxis of faith. I understand the Church as a fellowship of believers having kerygmatic (proclamation), koinonia (fellowship) and diakonic (serving the poor) mandate in this world. The material world requires physical involvement to activate the faith. It does happen through the physical experiences of people. Also, Church is the location where we learn and relearn the basics of faith and sometimes unlearn what is not of faith. Therefore, Church plays an important role in the spiritual journey of a Christian.

The Church welcomes believers into a fellowship that ought to embody the life of Jesus. It is the place where believers are reminded of the need of shaping their lives in tune with what Jesus taught and practiced. Sermons, testimonies, exhortations, and participation in worship help him/her to get deeply rooted in faith and develop a perspective that is informed by biblical revelation. The fellowship nature of the Church opens new avenues of sharing, caring and mutual empowerment regardless of caste, creed and class. Every event (physical) of biblical koinonia gives hope of new life to the participants. They derive energy from the fellowship to face the challenges in personal and societal life. It is this fellowship that makes the Christian faith a communitarian reality in which every individual practices faith by contributing to the life of a fellow believer. The Church stands for a community of faith that is characterized by the fellowship of believers who have covenantal relationships with Jesus and one another. The 'Word became Flesh' in order to have physical fellowship with humanity. The physicality of this event points to the need for the intimate fellowship of believers. Therefore, physical church life cannot be taken for granted under the pretext of the availability of online platforms and advanced technologies.

Like any other religious tradition, Christian faith is also known for its ethical system. Love is the basic ethical principle of Christian faith. It has two dimensions: one's love with God and with fellow beings (neighbors). The former is the extension of the latter. It does not happen in a vacuum but in a community. The Church is the basic unit where Christians begin to learn different dimensions of biblical love and concretely experience it. In this sense, the believers receive a new morality from the fellowship. It shapes their worldview and defines their identity: a community of love. The internalization and praxis of love bring them together and become a community through which the power of love flows and transforms the people.

The Church is not simply a physical structure but a community experience of faith through worship and sacraments. The nature of Christian worship and sacraments implies the physical presence of believers. Community experience of faith generates a sense of belonging among believers. It encourages them to come together and affirm what they believe. Though the individual experience of faith is crucial, its fullness comes from community participation. It is not a faceless but a face-to-face experience with God and fellow beings. This is important for the wholistic development of a believer's life. We need to focus on the community experience of faith in the Church than its structural or systemic advantages and disadvantages.

Many hesitate to go to Church not because it is irrelevant to them but because of its present life in society. For instance, the Church has become an institution today. Constitution and by-laws rule the Church than the Scripture and the community life of early Christians. An institutionalized Church does not bother much about community experience of faith. Here, individual obedience to the rules prevails over *koinonia, diakonia* and *kerygma*. It has created a new class of believers who restrict their church life to themselves. The Covid 19 pandemic has given them another reason to individualize Church life. For them, online worship is an alternative because they fail to understand and experience faith beyond their personal boundaries. Biblical faith does not endorse the 'individualization' of Church life. In fact, we have damaged the original image of the Church through the process of institutionalization.

The pandemic has taken us away from the physical church. Now, this is the time to go back to Church and reclaim its original image. We cannot think of our faith without its community experience. *Koinonia, diakonia* and *kerygma* are essential expressions of faith in the community. Church stands for it. Going to Church is not a 'ritual' but an experience of renewing our relationship with God and co-believers. While pandemic continues to normalize our societal life, it should not define our church life. Church life is a gift of God. We need to own it and care for it because it gives us identity, nurtures our faith and enables us to partake in the community of Jesus. Therefore, 'Back to Church' is essential for the believers to celebrate faith in a pandemic 'normal' context.

20

Ego Kills, Love Redeems

Ego means "a person's sense of self-esteem or self-importance." It becomes harmful when it negatively influences the self in interpersonal relationships and decision-making. Everyone has an ego. It manifests in the actions with varying degrees. However, it may also hurt as the body gets hurt daily. If the body hurts, we tend to ignore it, or we would be happy if we get 'sorry' from others. But if the ego gets hurt, we may not tolerate it unless it is satisfied by the befitting response to the source of hurt.

The human ego gets hurt for various reasons. For some, their ego will be hurt if their words are countered. For others, the ego will be hurt if their decisions are publicly challenged or questioned. Sometimes, the ego will be disturbed if the person feels that s/he is disrespected. For many, ego is hurt if they are overlooked. At times, ego shows up if s/he is not taken into consideration in a particular situation. Ego is also hurt if s/he is unable to fulfill the promise or achieve the target as expected. Occasionally, one's body language can make another person's ego hurt. The problem with 'touch-me-not-ego' is that s/he never knows what consequences his/her 'hurt' ego will bring into his/ her life or others' lives.

One of the consequences is that s/he may withhold good from those who deserve it. According to Bible, "Do not withhold good from those who deserve it, when it is in your power to act" (Pro 3: 28). Often, we release good to a person who does not deserve it and withhold the same from the person who deserves it. Ego determines the destiny of action at this juncture.

All are powerful in one or the other way. Power has contextual character. Some will have limited power, others absolute power in a particular situation. Some are administratively powerful; some are powerful in terms of money, knowledge, leadership, contact etc. We can use the power to withhold 'good' from others or release the energy that will bring change in life or enable a person to celebrate his/her life in its fullness. When power is used to withhold good from a person who deserves it or to satisfy one's ego, then it can be termed as misuse or abuse of power.

Our ego can kill us and others. When we withhold good from a person, we kill his/her opportunities, prospects, and blessings in life. Sometimes it may cause the death of a person. When we do it, often we do not realize that we are dead in the sight of God. We invite God to withhold our blessing even though we deserve it. In its operation, the ego produces a victimizer and a victim. Both experience the consequences of ego. Therefore, both need freedom: the victimizer requires freedom from an egoistic mindset and its immediate effect on his or her life, and the victim longs for freedom from the egoistic actions of the victimizer.

A Christian cannot withhold good from others because s/ he is a new creation in Christ who emptied himself and lived as an egoless person. During baptism, a believer has emptied his/her ego and become a new creation. S/he must live as an egoless person because of his/her identity as the disciple of Jesus Christ. As a new creation, s/he is an embodiment of love, but not of ego. Even if the ego is hurt, s/he cannot withhold any form of good from others because his/her life subsists in Christ. Christ was hurt many times, but he loved everyone and did not withhold good, particularly the greatest 'good' to the world, salvation. But we continue to hurt him by swimming in the muddy waters of ego. He continues to shower his goodness upon humanity.

Christ is the reason for us not to withhold good from others. If Christ has not withheld good from humanity, continues to protect us, and put us in responsible positions or whatever way we are powerful, we have no right or authority to withhold 'good' from anyone. Our ego sometimes has the power of a 'nuclear bomb' that can affect the person or family or community for generations.

What is the solution if the ego of a person kills another; particularly it compels a person to withhold good from others.

Love is the solution. Biblical love is redemptive love. It has the power to redeem the victims of the egoist mindset. Redemptive love needs to be reflected in liberating actions. While revenge will flow out from the egoistic mind, redemptive actions will gush out from the mind of love as water gushes out from the reservoir. Whereas the letters of discouragement may come out of an egoistic pen, the letters of life that will make the dead alive may come out of the pen of love. Egoistic actions give birth to enemies, but the actions of love channelize transformative energy that flows from the cross and penetrate to the stony hearts. The human ego can destroy a community, church/institution/

relationship but love can build up a person, community, family etc. Ego is a life-negating force that demands satisfaction by withholding good from others. Love is a life-affirming power that seeks delight in liberating individuals from the clutches of ego and its consequences.

Jesus showed us the paradigm. He buried his ego with his baptism. His ego must also have been tested during temptation. The beauty of Jesus' life is that the ego could not stop the flow of love from his life. When he was challenged, he exhibited his love. When he was questioned, he answered in love. When he was disrespected, he behaved in love. When he was threatened, he appeared calm. It means ego should be countered by love. To be faithful and fruitful in Christian life and ministry the ego must be killed, and love must be manifested through actions. A Christian should always be reminded of the fact that ego kills but love redeems!

21

Friend's Wound and Enemy's Kiss

Faithful are the wounds of a friend; but kisses of an enemy are deceitful (Proverbs 27:6)

We do not want anyone to offend us, challenge us or question us. We always like to stay with people who are comfortable and pleasant to us in every circumstance. Therefore, we keep this criterion while choosing friends. Even if they confront us for the right reasons, we suddenly disassociate with them and treat them differently. Humans tend to define friendship from the perspective of comfort, convenience, and compliance. In friendship, for many, disagreement is tolerable, but questioning his or her decisions, prejudicial attitude etc. strains the relationship. It leads one to accuse another of wounding his/her psyche.

In friendship, can a friend wound us? Sometimes, we feel wounded by friends. We express it by saying that 'I am hurt.' The words, actions, and silence of our friends may cause our wounds. We do not expect such wounds from them because we believe that they cannot hurt us. We emotionally react to the surprise of the wound from friends. For most of us questioning is one of the sources of wounds. Disagreement also hurt us. Mostly, friendships turn into enmity because of the differences in opinions. A slight difference in body language leads to the temptation of suspicion and becomes a potential threat to the trust built over years.

In life and career, we come across two types of friends: firstly, a true, real, and genuine friend, and secondly, a friend but an enemy (friend-cum-enemy). Both are friends but different in their approaches, motives, and strategies. They are part of our lives. They travel with us and share our personal and public space. The problem with most of us is that we fail to discern who is 'real' among them. We define their loyalty based on how they positively respond to what we think and affirm. It may have ideological or religious reasons too.

A real friend may not agree with all our decisions. S/he chastises us, contests our thinking, and appreciates our integrity. S/he may question us when we are on the wrong track. S/he gives us face-to-face encounters and timely advice. S/he does not stab from behind but point fingers at our flaws. His/her approach is affirmative and productive. S/he stays with us without benefits. S/he expects the least and attempts for the best in us. S/he knows our mind and celebrates our success and shares our pain. S/he does not misuse friendship and exploit our vulnerabilities. S/he does not abandon us but stands with us in time of crisis. His/her motive is to protect us from impending perils that arise from our wrong choices and conclusions. His/her encounters always direct us to the right path, which leads toward fruitfulness. His/her disagreement is not a sign of unfaithfulness but a divine intervention that shapes our thinking and reroutes our journey. His/her approach may hurt us and inflict wounds. They are not real wounds but signs of true friendship.

A friend but enemy agrees with us in everything: our opinions, decisions, actions, and convictions. It is his /her 'kiss' to us. S/he appears to be willing to do anything for us. Like a friend s/he walks with us, eats with us, and shares our space. But s/he accompanies us with a different motive. His/her ultimate aim is to get what is available to us and push us into trouble. His/her agreement is a double-edged sword. While it gives him/her temporary privileges, it draws the friend closer to destruction. S/he plans and uses a friend's proximity to accomplish his/her goals. S/he does not correct us but encourages us to continue in the pathway. S/he has a double face: a pleasant face before us and a spiteful face before others when s/he talks about us. S/he stays with us as long as we can keep him/her in good humor. The strategy of the enemy is to kiss. We never doubt him/her because s/he gives us both physical and symbolic kiss (approval, support) as a token of loyalty and love. Kisses are not always a sign of true friendship. We value the kiss of 'friend-cum-enemy' over the wound of a real friend who encounters us with questions, pieces of advice, and disagreements.

The wound of a friend may be painful, but it will be healed quickly. It is not fatal. It has inherent healing power. A real friend may 'offend' us but there is hidden positive redemptive value in the apparent offense. We consider it a wound because we deceive ourselves with our 'self-conviction' that we are always right: we take the right decisions, deliver the right judgments, chart the right journey, and select the right people. The wounds we endure because of our real friend's disagreements and corrections will be healed when we realize that s/he is right in evaluating us at a particular time. We need to cultivate openness, a tolerant attitude, and critical consciousness to reach the stage of realizing that we are wrong. Every human being is subject to correction. Who corrects us? Christians believe that God or the Word of

God corrects us. It happens through people who are close to us. A friend is the best tool to correct us.

'Kiss' by a friend-cum-enemy is pleasant but poisonous for a longer period. It leads us into problems. Unlike a real friend, 'friend-cum-enemy' kisses to destroy us. S/he always longs to kiss us with lovely words and proximity. We enjoy his /her 'kiss' in the form of approval or agreement with our mistakes or wrong judgments without realizing the poison of enmity ingrained in the kiss. S/he who realizes the hidden negative potential of the enemy's kiss saves his/her life. As long as we are ensnared by the 'kiss' of the enemy, we do not respond to the voice of a real friend. We ignore his/her voice because we feel that it irritates us and discourages us. The story of 'friend-cum-enemy' ends with the tragedy in which s/he deserts us and celebrates our fall.

Everyone needs someone in his/her life to offend, challenge, and question. Only a true friend can do this job with good intention. We should not be afraid of his/her disagreement with us. It will refine us, purify us and correct us for a better tomorrow. It can be a family member, a colleague, a childhood friend, a life partner, etc. S/he will not 'kiss' us like an enemy, but journey with us like a beacon that signals the right path. A wound from a friend has redemptive value. His/her questions, criticism and advice may hurt us, but they can save us from danger. The questions may hurt us, but it is worth enduring. There are two choices in friendship: a real friend and a friend but an enemy. One may give occasional wounds and other frequent kisses. The Bible values the wounds of a friend than the kisses of an enemy. A Christian should consider *"faithful are the wounds of a friend, but kisses of an enemy are deceitful."* It's not the wound, but what it serves matters.

22

Temptation

The word 'temptation' means "desire to do something, especially something wrong or unwise." It is part of human life to be tempted for right or wrong reasons. It happens to everyone, irrespective of age, gender, class, and creed. Though there may be commonalities in the manifestations of temptation, we experience them in different levels and realms due to our contextual particularities. We face it in relation to work, ministry, finance, power, fame, sexuality, and interpersonal relationships. Linguistically, 'temptation' has negative traits: the temptation to usurp power, to compromise faith or integrity, to leave the ministry or job, to fight for petty causes, to argue for no reason, to be lazy, etc. But 'temptation' can be decorated with positive vibes also. Instead of negative temptation, we should talk about positive temptation. We should tempt to love the unloved, build up the relationship amid brokenness, establish peace in the midst of conflicts, identify with those in crisis, help others, cultivate proactive behavior in the atmosphere of negativity, to release positive energy, and nurture a liberative attitude. By redefining the word, 'temptation,' with positive actions, we can redeem it from the bondage of 'negativity.' The redefinition of 'temptation' may build up personal and community life. However, the 'beauty' of negative temptation is that it is not altogether practically negative.

While temptation with negative intent has the power to destroy a person if s/he succumbs to it, it can contribute to constructing a person if s/he resists its negative import. The negativity attached to temptation should be countered by the positivity 'hidden' in it. Jesus' experience of temptation (Matt 4: 1-11) offers some insights to overcome the negative intention and destructive energy of the temptation. According to the story narrated in the Gospel of Matthew, the devil tempted Jesus to perform a miracle (turning stones into bread), jump from the highest point of the temple, and worship the devil. It was a temptation of power, position, and possession. Jesus discerned the negativity involved in the temptation and he used the opportunity to prove himself against the devil's strategy. Throughout his ministry, Jesus confronted negative temptation and activated positive temptation to build up individuals.

Discernment of Temptation

Human beings have a natural capacity to discern temptation and its consequences. It may vary from person to person. While some attempt to discern temptation and respond to it within the framework of ideologies, others depend on ethical and doctrinal systems of religions. Discernment of temptation is the first step to counter its negative impact. Human beings succumb to temptation because they either fail to discern its negative impact timely or willfully ignore it even though they know its consequences. For Christians, the Word of God (Scripture) is the framework to discern the signs of negative temptation. In the story of temptation, Jesus discerned the temptation of the devil.

His answer to each temptation underlines the fact that Scripture is the basis to discern the temptation. He also displayed how to discern the negative temptation that contradicts the Scripture. The Word of God provides guiding principles for Christians to discern what is right and wrong. They shape the thinking and actions of a Christian. S/he cannot randomly decide and respond according to his/her momentary feeling. S/he cannot accept or reject an appeal or a request or a challenge based on his/her circumstances. It should be evaluated in light of the Scripture. Anything that contradicts the teachings of Scripture falls into the category of negative temptation. For a Christian, the Scripture prevails over his/her mind and consciousness. Scripture helps him/her to discern temptation and overcome it.

Method of Resistance

The story of the temptation of Jesus provides a glimpse of the method to resist negative temptation. It tells us that negative temptation can be resisted. It gives hope to those who are victimized by negative temptation. Jesus resisted temptation by proclaiming what is written in the Scripture. The proclamation of the Word has the power to challenge the strategies of Satan. His answer to each temptation came from Scripture. It explains that internalization of the Word of God can overcome the power of temptation. The internalization of God's Word empowers us to proclaim it over the snares of temptation. Jesus resisted the temptation of position, power, and possession by affirming the sovereignty of God in the Scripture. Jesus' method calls for praxis in life. The temptation of enmity should be resisted by the principle of love described in the Scripture. The temptation of disobedience should be resisted by the biblical value of obedience. The temptation of bribes should be resisted by the biblical teaching against bribes. Justice should be proclaimed over injustice. Equality should be proclaimed over inequality. Biblical servanthood should resist the temptation of superior consciousness. The biblical teaching of freedom should be declared over the temptation to negate freedom. Scripture does not endorse discrimination, division, exclusion, and domination. But we are tempted to discriminate against people, create divisions, exclude or devalue people, and dominate others. Jesus' experience of temptation gives the motivation to overcome temptations in life. While temptation is human, resistance to temptation is a biblical mandate. For Christians, Jesus is the model for resisting temptation and the Scripture is the source of resistance.

Test of Commitment

In the story of temptation, Jesus did not run away from the temptation of the devil but boldly faced it. The devil could not succeed to entice Jesus even though the challenge was not difficult for Jesus. He realized that it was a temptation that came from the devil. His identity does not derive from being obedient to the devil but from being resistant to the devil. By overcoming temptation, Jesus proved his identity (derived from God) and proclaimed his trust in God who sent him to this world. His experience of temptation was a time of a test that revealed his commitment to the mission. He defeated the power of temptation and began his redemptive mission. The experience of temptation established him as a person competent to take up the divine mission of human salvation. It means temptation reveals a person's aptitude for a particular mission. A person's commitment to his/her vision and mission also is made known through the test of temptation. As temptation proved who Jesus was, so we should take it as an opportunity to demonstrate who we are. Response to temptation speaks about a person's commitment to the ideologies, values, and beliefs s/he adheres to. We may advocate against corruption, but our commitment to honesty is tested at the time of financial crisis in life. Many people value transparency in public life but their commitment to transparency is tested when they are scrutinized. Jesus showed us how committed he was to himself (personal convictions) and God at the time of temptation. His life embodied his commitment to the values he taught and stood for. The test in the desert took him to another place of his commitment: Calvary where he finally defeated the power of temptation. He could have been tempted by the desire to avoid the cross. But his commitment led him to choose the cross over the temptation.

Testimony out of Temptation

There is a potential testimony in temptation. It depends on how we conform to or resist temptation. Resistance to temptation produces testimony. In the Christian language, it is a witness to the faith experience in life. Testimony that emerges out of temptation describes a person's character, quality, commitment and convictions. The experience of temptation became a testimony to Jesus' life and ministry. It gave him a credible foundation for his future ministry. It also made him confident to proceed with his mission. Testimony has the power to renew oneself and others. For instance, Jesus' testimony of overcoming temptation continues to strengthen people in crisis. While resistance to temptation generates testimony, submission to temptation offers temporal gratification for the self. Testimony enriches the community of faith, whereas surrender to temptation destroys it. We should translate temptation into testimony. The temptation of power should give way to the testimony of service. Being ethical in thinking and action is a testimony of resistance to the temptation of being corrupt and immoral. Testimony starts where temptation loses its power. This is possible if we discern negative temptation and resist it with the Word of God.

23

Change not by Human Power but by God's Spirit

Humans strive to be powerful where they are located. They claim solutions to every problem because they presume that they are mighty in every sense. They possess power, be it military, technological, economic, or political. They believe that they can change any situation and achieve any goal with power. In that process, the power speaks a different language, mainly the language of dominance. Therefore, the powerful embodies the language of dominance. Power makes them confident that they can initiate a change. They use different tools and strategies to usher in change. Unfortunately, the change/transformation they proclaim is biased and exclusive. It does not have an egalitarian view. It has victims and victors. The powerful are not the apostles of holistic change through fair means but advocates of a new order which proclaims the Mighty is Right. They are seen in political, social, and religious communities. Today's world acknowledges the people who are powerful or have access to the corridors of power because it is taught that they alone can bring change. It also defines the powerful in terms of money, race, class, caste, etc. Christian faith defines the powerful as those who are led by the power and the fruits of God's spirit (Galatians 5: 22). The powerful are not those who can dominate and forcibly transform people but serve and lead them into the horizons of change. Christian life calls for an intentional engagement intended to prepare individuals and communities for a transformed life in this world. Christianity advocates progressive change in human life in line with the teachings of Jesus Christ. It happens not by human power but by the Spirit of God (Zachariah 4:6).

Christianity affirms that God is Almighty. Human beings are God's creation and instruments to change the world into God's Kingdom. God intervenes in history through human beings. They are finite beings who derive strength from God. But humans misunderstand the source of their 'power,' and depend on money, physical strength, and socio-political-economic networks. The powerful, for God, is not muscular, wealthy, and dominant people but those who listen to the Spirit of God and activate the power of God through the fruits of God's Spirit. They channelize divine energy to transform individuals and communities. It happens in ministry, workplaces and public spaces. We are participants in the process of the divine plan of cosmic transformation. We cooperate with God, the Almighty, who empowers us to become the beacon of change in the locations of darkness, discrimination, exclusion and pain. The powerful of this world may not go into such location because they are not 'really' powerful to encounter the broken realities of human life. It is possible only with the people empowered by the Spirit of God. Every Christian is powerful because of the Spirit of God.

The powerful, in Christian language, are servants but not masters who misuse power for vested interests. They are powerful because they are courageous to love the unlovable.

Their actions change the mindset of the dominant and give a new life to those in the periphery. The actions of love bring the margins into the centre. This is a change of location and status. The powerful enables others to celebrate life in its fullness. They live for the joy of others as Jesus did. They are peace-makers, not peace-breakers. They are patient listeners to the victimized and oppressed in society. They are compassionate to respond to the needy and the poor. They spread the fragrance of goodness in the community. They uphold integrity and resist the temptations of power and wealth. They have control over their thoughts, speeches, and actions. They embrace everyone. They are powerful not by their might but by the Spirit (*BERUHI*, Zachariah 4:6). Christian faith teaches that change happens not by might but by nurturing and demonstrating the fruits of the Spirit in actions. This is the meaning of *BERUHI* today. Christian life is a witness to *BERUHI*. Christianity is a kerygmatic community of *BERUHI*. Christian mission/ministry is an actualization of *BERUHI*. The history of Christianity proves it. *BERUHI* is a strong reminder against the institutionalized, hierarchical, casteist, and patriarchal Christian community boastful of its denominational strength, financial resources and political clout. *BERUHI* invites us to be empowered by the Spirit of God to empower the disempowered in society. *BERUHI* is also a theological challenge to shift our dependence and framework of actions: from human power to the Spirit of God. The change that happens through the Spirit of God is a liberating and enduring experience. Christians are stewards of this change.

24

Integrity

Today, integrity has become a rare commodity in society. People talk about integrity in their sermons, lectures, motivational speeches, and daily conversations but do not practice it in real life. They tend to compromise their integrity for temporary gratification. The 'words' of human beings have also lost their credibility in interpersonal relationships because they do not keep their words or promises. Many are not stable in their opinions and decisions. Therefore, suspicion has crept into every human relationship though its impact varies from case to case. People have no qualms about changing their words and go into denial mode. Everyone experiences the issue of trust deficit in different spheres of life. It has become normal for human beings to witness the drama of 'promise and withdrawal.' For instance, we come across people who offer something today and change their words for trivial reasons tomorrow. For them, survival outweighs integrity in their personal and professional lives. They do not feel guilty about building up their career at the cost of integrity. Their words and works are incompatible. But the virtue of integrity does not allow a person to compromise his/her values. It is a mark of a bold person.

R. Raman has written a beautiful article, "The Post Ideology Politician" (*The Indian Express* 9 March 2022). According to him, we live in a post-ideology context where power is the essence of life. Ideology, political commitment, and loyalty are variables. Recently, some political parties asked their candidates to sign affidavits or take oaths in the places of worship so that they would not change their allegiance after the electoral victory. The crisis of integrity is not limited to politicians. It has taken root among all sections of humanity. In line with R. Raman, I would say that we live in a post-faith context. Religion and morality no longer shape our views and decisions as they influenced us in the past. Religious identity has become superficial in the sense that it does not reflect in the behaviour of people. Many do not feel guilty when they break what their religion or ideology has taught them. For instance, a person may tell a lie; still, s/he is a 'Christian.' S/he may swindle money; still, s/he is a 'Christian.' S/he is not Christian but claims so. S/he has no problem in breaking promises; still s/he claims religiosity. Ideological commitment has given way to ideological masking. Indeed, we live in a world of a credibility crisis. In this context, the words of Jesus, "Simply let your 'Yes' be 'Yes,' and your 'No,' 'No;' anything beyond this comes the evil one" (Matthew 5: 37) remind us about the importance of integrity.

Integrity means the "quality of being honest and having strong moral principles." A person of integrity lives by the values s/he upholds in life. For Christians, life values come from the Scripture, particularly the life and teachings of Jesus Christ. In the passage (Matthew 5: 33-37), although an oath is allowed in OT, Jesus takes the issue of taking an oath to a new level by denying the necessity of an oath altogether. A person's word can be relied on without an oath. Here, Jesus introduces a new standard of ethics. A person's 'yes' must be really 'yes' and 'no' really 'no.' The issue is all about integrity. It talks about the integrity of a person's life as a whole. What is implied in the words of Jesus is that an honest person does not need to take an oath. Swearing points to the vulnerability of a person's integrity and the possibility of going away from his/her 'Yes' or 'No.' The oath requires in the context of lack of trust between persons.

Integrity Demands Our Yes be Yes; No be No

Some people change their 'yes' or 'no' as casually as they change their clothes . Today's 'yes' becomes tomorrow's 'no' and vice versa. For them, the distance between 'yes' and 'no' is very short. They take less time to change their views. They do not think about the consequences of their change of words in their lives and others' lives. The problem with such people is that they are not shaped by any ideology or faith. They have no hesitation in selling their minds for temporary benefits. 'Compromise,' not 'commitment,' is the mark of their private and public life. Money can convert their 'yes' into 'no'; 'no' into 'yes.' An offer of position can swiftly change their 'no' into 'yes.' They are ideologically weak and virtually dangerous to the community and relationships. God knows the feeble nature of the human mind. Therefore, Jesus demands integrity from every human being. Integrity demands us to be consistent in our perspectives, opinions and actions. The framework of our actions should be consistent and productive. 'Yes,' and 'no' of a Christian should be defined by the Word of God. The language of 'Yes' and 'no' (integrity) is not a language of rigidity or orthodoxy but of consistency, reliability, and truth.

Integrity Calls for Accountability

Integrity requires accountability from a person for his/her action. Some do not own his/her action if it does not yield the expected result. Others retreat from their convictions when they feel that they are wrong in the sight of people even though they are right. They forget the fact that the majority is not always right. Integrity does not allow a person to run away from or disown his/her actions or the positions s/he has taken. Whether it is good or bad in the eyes of people, s/he should stand on the ground and fight for his/her conviction. For Christians, a person's conviction on what is right or wrong is determined by their faith. An action out of conviction reflects the integrity of a person. A person with integrity boldly owns what s/he said publicly or privately. For example, s/he will say, "I said about you," "I said that" or "I did it." S/he does blame others. S/he stands strong even when anything happens contrary to his/her values or expectations. S/he does not switch sides. S/he cannot be neutral when the situation calls him/her to be honest. Integrity calls for him/her to take a side because his/her 'Yes' or 'No' makes a difference in a particular situation. Neutral people are not responsible and do not contribute to life.

Integrity Resists Temptation

People encounter different kinds of temptations. One of them is the temptation to compromise integrity. It happens in personal, familial, public spaces, and interpersonal relationships. Many are least concerned about integrity when it comes to power, authority, and wealth. They change their 'yes' or 'no' according to the situation, particularly if it quenches their thirst for power. They are opportunists and the victims of temptations. But people with integrity are always guided by the principles of faith. They may not succumb to temptations. They value honesty at the cost of losing comfort, privilege, and fame. They discern the voice of temptation and resist it with spiritual and moral capital. Integrity has the power to defeat temptation. If a person changes his/

her 'yes' or 'no' at the point of temptation, that is the work of the devil. It is evil to change the words of promise. Integrity is divine, but the compromise of integrity is demonic. Jesus is the model for integrity in life. Integrity is one of the hallmarks of a Christian in this world.

25

The Seed Bearers of Change

Every human being has ambitions in life. Some pursue their goals with determination and enthusiasm. They are optimistic in their approach and attempt to achieve their goals against any odd situations. They boldly take up the task and explore the possibilities to accomplish it. Others are pessimistic and more skeptical about the outcome of their efforts. It makes them dormant in life. They do not venture out into new terrain of possibilities. They are afraid to take steps that catapult them into another level of life or career or ministry. They are unaware that they have potential and are seed bearers of change. The Bible tells many stories, particularly miracles that motivate people to come out of the ghetto of pessimism. Often, we read them only from the point of view of supernatural intervention. They also give us insights to activate human agency to participate in miracles and become beacons of change. The story of Jesus' miracle of feeding the five thousand in the Bible (John 6: 1-14) is a case in point.

In this story, a huge crowd followed Jesus, probably to see or experience His miraculous acts. While sitting with his disciples on a mountainside, Jesus asked Philip, one of his disciples, "Where shall we buy bread for these people to eat?" The location might be far off from a commercial place. Philip answered, "Eight months' wages would not buy enough bread for each one to have a bite." Andrew, another disciple, probably explored the possibility and found a boy with "five small barley loaves and two small fish." But he was skeptical about the practicality of feeding the crowd with limited provisions. Jesus took the loaves and fish and thanked (prayed) and distributed them to the crowd. Five thousand of them were men. Everyone had sufficient food to eat. In the end, the disciples collected twelve baskets of leftover barley loaves. The crowd witnessed a miraculous act of Jesus and called him the Prophet whom they anticipated. Though this story narrates a miracle, it has a message for the people who are gripped by negative thinking and fear of failure.

Negative Thinking/Mind Restricts the Space

Philip represents negative or narrow-minded people. They are cynics who find no possibility for a new venture. They are prisoners of existing conditions. They do not envision beyond where/what they are. They write conclusions within the framework of survival. Their minds are always conditioned by negativities and doubts. Indeed, they love the status quo and take refuge in present reality. They blame circumstances as obstacles to enlarging their space. They are also content with what they have achieved. Instead of spreading the fragrance of positive thinking, they live with a negative mind. They are not conscious that negativity (negative thinking) not only restricts their space but also impacts the lives of others. Negativity is not biblical because God does not endorse negative thinking. It is a human way of thinking as Philip calculated for the expense of Jesus' proposal of feeding the crowd from an economic point of view. The calculation is not wrong, but the attitude behind it restricts the potential to venture out. A negative attitude does not help fulfill a dream. Every new initiative comes from a strong vision that transcends the present situation. It needs a positive mind to accomplish it.

There is another companion to positive thinking: faith. For Christians, though we should take up any task with a positive mind, we should always be aware that God makes it successful. They affirm faith in God along with positive thinking. Positive thinking should be shaped by biblical faith and values. God does not entrust any responsibility or assignment without ensuring the resources needed to achieve it. We need to take it up with commitment and faith in God. If change is desired in life, career, and ministry, we should cherish and cultivate positive thinking. While negative thinking restricts the space, positive thinking with faith in God enlarges it.

An Exploring Mind: Capital to Achieve the Goal

Jesus' question might have encouraged Andrew to explore the possibility. He did not succumb to the snare of doubt. He represents people with an exploring mind today. They are not discouraged by the questions, challenges, and tasks. They always explore the possibilities to achieve their goal because they possess positive thinking. An exploring mind produces positive energy. It can break new pathways to reach the destination. People with an exploring mind do not dwell in the present condition forever. For them, an exploring mind is a capital, not money. Only bold people can explore because it is risky, time-consuming, and sometimes painful. They are not afraid of failure but are focused on their goals. They go from pillar to post to get their tasks completed. Andrew must have searched for the provisions without fear of failure. An exploring mind does not pause even if it meets failure. It overcomes the obstacles on the way to realizing the goals. Discouragement does not stop the journey of an exploring mind. Change happens through an exploring mind. In other words, change does not come if we do not take the risk of exploring the possibilities. Christian faith adds a 'faith dimension' to the exploring mind. Faith and hard work/ an exploring mind help us to reach the phase of accomplishment. The exploring mind of Andrew contributed to the goal (miracle) of feeding five thousand. He used his exploring mind and participated in the process of achieving the goal. He also became instrumental in channelizing divine favour in a remote location.

Know the Potential and Participate in the Miracle

According to the story, a boy was also part of the crowd. He had five small barley loaves and two small fish. But he did not know that food in his hands would feed the entire crowd. For me, five small barley loaves and two small fish symbolize the potential of every human being. Many become pessimists because they do not know their potential in them. In order to achieve goals and experience change in life (miracle), a person should be conscious of his/her potential. This boy was ignorant of the power of his potential. The consciousness of potential gives the courage to venture out and participate in the process of a miracle of change. The consciousness of the potential alone does not help to accomplish the goal. It should be expressed or activated. I imagine that when Andrew approached the boy, he showed Andrew what was in his hand. I would symbolically take his gesture as a bold expression of a person's potential. Public display of one's potential also opens new opportunities in life and enlarges one's space. Christian faith teaches the virtue of sharing. Therefore, a person's potential does not exclusively belong to him/her but to the community/society, s/he belongs. Change (miracle) happens when a person is willing to share his/her potential with others. The boy might have wholeheartedly given his tiffin box to Andrew. By doing so, he not only shared his potential but also participated in the miracle. The story also explains how the potential was multiplied. It means, along with the consciousness of potential, expression of potential, and readiness to share the potential, the knowledge of the source/means of multiplication of potential is also essential to participate in the miracle. Christian faith teaches that Jesus is the source of the multiplication of potential/resources. A person needs to release his/her potential and define the life journey. The limited potential is not a justifiable reason to abstain from an event of a miracle. Everyone is a partaker in miracles because s/he has potential which can be multiplied for a greater purpose.

Jesus: Model for Bold Initiatives in Unexpected Locations

In this episode, Jesus may be a performer of miracles for the crowd. However, he communicates a different message to the people who are timid to take bold initiatives in unexpected locations. Jesus asked his disciples to arrange bread for the crowd who followed him. I assume that it was an unexpected demand for his disciples at that point in time, particularly in a remote location. Jesus took a bold decision to provide bread for the people. He did not take the situation into consideration or the practicality of his question. The condition of people might have influenced his decision. Throughout his ministry, Jesus had a compassionate attitude towards common people and met their immediate needs. In this story, he multiplied the available resources and shared them with the people. He was not influenced by Philip's pessimistic observation of the situation. Today, Jesus stands as a model for envisioning and implementing innovative ideas in a dry and barren location. He also tells us that God performs wonders in unexpected terrains. How we respond to the question of Jesus or our vision matters for experiencing the miracle. In other words, how do we respond to the remote locations in life and ministry? While some may imitate Philip, others attempt to explore the possibility. But Jesus encourages us to boldly envision and take initiatives in dry locations where people long for quenching their social and spiritual thirst. It transforms dry locations into locations of celebrating God's Glory. Every location offers a variety of possibilities. Christians believe that God is the source of every bold initiative. God empowers a person to be bold in thinking and uses him/her to change the condition of a location. This location may be a geographical, social, economic, or political condition. S/he, having a bold vision, stays with people and feeds them in unexpected ways. Bold initiatives change the destiny of people. They are no longer the people of dry locations but of celebrating their lives in fullness.

Change the Perspective

People use a different lens to evaluate a situation, an individual's potential, resources, opportunities, and challenges and act upon them. How do we look defines the future too. Take the main characters in the story. Philip looked at the situation and the crowd and concluded that it was not possible at that point in time. Andrew with his exploring mind looked differently and observed that it was not altogether impossible. He saw at least one sign of possibility but was not fully confident. The small boy had a different outlook. Though he did not know the potential of what he was carrying, he shared it with others. He might have thought that if his tiffin box helps Jesus to feed the crowd, then, let this happen. The crowd, I imagine, without knowing what Jesus was contemplating, was patiently waiting for him to perform his 'usual' miracle. Jesus had a different perspective informed by his concern for common people including children and a bold vision of transforming people's thinking, faith, and location. Jesus calls for everyone to change the perspective that has a limited vision and action. Change happens when we alter our way of looking at possibilities. We should look through the lens of Jesus who saw a miracle in a remote location. Jesus' perspective brings forth bold initiatives. The shift in perspective leads a person to participate in the miracle. It should be guided by the life and work of Jesus. Instead of looking at present situations and limited resources through the lens of ideologies, we should look at them through the eyes of Jesus to see hidden possibilities. When an exploring mind and limited potential meet Jesus, change happens, a miracle occurs, and blessing flows from one person to the crowd. Jesus multiplies the limited potential/ resources by changing our perspective and enhancing our faith in God. Every human being carries a seed of change. S/he is a seed bearer of change. S/he should allow the seed (potential) to grow. Sometimes, its growth requires a shift in perspective. The seed grows into a tree which gives fruits and shadow to people. Our limited potential should be multiplied to provide a shadow to the multitude who expects miracles in their lives.

26

Call and Consequences

Some Realities

According to Christian faith, God calls people for ministry and consecrates them with specific gifts to accomplish different ministerial purposes. While some believe that everyone receives God's calling, others limit God's calling to chosen individuals. People receive the call of God through different means and experiences. God's call comes to people through the Word of God, the ministry of a prophet, dreams, personal conviction, parents (dedicating children to ministry), personal encounters with God, etc. Some people have decided to engage in ministry purely out of their personal interest. This can also be considered one of the ways through which God calls a person into ministry. I believe that a follower of Christ is a servant of God who has a divine calling to participate in the mission of God. The nature and location of ministry may be different but s/he is an equal participant in Christian ministry at large. S/he is a believer, a minister, and a missionary. S/he is answerable to God in responding to the call in the context where s/he is placed. In this reflection, I specifically focus on the ministerial call of pastors, missionaries, and leaders of the Church because the clergy occupies the ministerial space in the present Church. Often, they misunderstand their calling and mislead the laity and monopolize the sacramental power. A theological reminder of biblical calling may help the laity and the clergy internalize the essence and praxis of calling.

Every call comes with a purpose though ultimately, it is an invitation to serve Jesus. We receive the call of God and try to activate it in a context that is competitive, challenging, authoritarian, and individualistic. Sometimes, we are encouraged to celebrate the calling, but at times we are also discouraged to see the abuse or misuse of calling in the lives of many self-claimed, anointed servants of the Lord! They do not realize the fact that they are called to represent Jesus and his ministry in this world. Unfortunately, many are constrained to activate their call experiences in the churches/denominations, institutions, organizations, and mission fields led or controlled by the mediocre, selfish, and power-mongering bishops, presidents, principals, institutional heads, etc. The leaders willfully forget their calling to indulge in dirty politics and seize power.

Church is called the body of Christ. Today, many churches and institutions are corrupt or smelly 'bodies.' They do not manifest the beauty of Jesus' compassion in the ministry and the valour of Jesus on the Cross. They are 'smelly' bodies not because of the sweat of the hard labour, but because of the unchristian behavior of 'called' leaders. In the past, we had self-sacrificing leaders who nurtured people's calling, but now we have leaders who extinguish the fire of calling. However, there are remnants whose life and ministry continue to influence many young men and women to take up the Cross of Jesus. They give hope to the future Church.

Today, calling has been reduced to a means to get a job or a position in churches or institutions. In the name of calling, many of us place mundane demands before Jesus than receive orders from him. By seeing the life of many 'called servants,' God must be 'regretting' to call them. Do we belong to this category? For example, I belong to the ministry category of theological educators. Often, they criticize the condition of the Church, particularly the behavior of the leaders of the Church. They appear to be true prophets in the classrooms and Chapel pulpits. However, some of them also seek the support of 'corrupt' leaders to accomplish their ambitions. They also play politics; devise plans to get power and privileges. Sadly, most of us have lost our call consciousness. In the place of call consciousness, we have chair consciousness, power consciousness and leader consciousness. The moment we lose call-consciousness, corruption, division, and all 'isms' (casteism, regionalism, nepotism, denominationalism) get into our psyche and the psyche of the churches and institutions. The administrative, leadership, spiritual, missional, and ministry crises that we witness in Indian Churches and Christian institutions is the result of the lack of call consciousness. Does it mean that we have lost everything? No! We need to reclaim our call-consciousness. How do we reclaim our call consciousness? Go back to the call of Jesus. What is the nature of Jesus' call?

Jesus' Call

Jesus called people to join his mission. The idea of Jesus' call can be derived from the events narrated in the Bible (Matthew 4: 18-22, 9:9; Mark 2: 13-14, 3: 13-19, 6: 6-13 and Luke 5: 1-11 & 27). Unlike a Jewish Rabbi, Jesus called his disciples to follow him. In fact, his disciples were not choosing and staying with him as Paul studied under Gamaliel (Acts 22: 3). Ancient

India also had the same style of master-disciple relationship called *gurukulam*. The nature and purpose of Jesus' call were different from other teachers who accepted disciples to study the Scripture and law. Jesus did not call them to have a life of rigorous study and become conventional religious teachers but to proclaim his message and participate in a mission journey that had dangerous trajectories. Jesus' life and ministry inform us of the nature and essence of his call.

Jesus' call was risky in his context and has the same impact even today. It called for sacrifice, brokenness, and solidarity with the people in the periphery. It was a call to live for others. It placed the disciples in hostile locations and put their lives under frequent threats. But the power of Jesus' call was such that the disciples did not retreat from the task of proclaiming and practicing the message of the Kingdom of God. They internalized the call of Jesus strongly and faced the challenges bravely. The biblical accounts and legends inform us that most of them had violent deaths. They were faithful to their calling at the cost of their lives. Their call was risky because of the liberating and revolutionary content of the message of Jesus. It challenged the structures of power and invoked the values of justice, equality, freedom, and peace. In the context of the purity-pollution laws, economic and social disparity, male normativity, and feudalistic mindset, Jesus called his disciples to deconstruct the thinking and the attitude of people. It was also a call to serve everyone and enable them to celebrate life in its fullness. Jesus did not call his disciples to become theoreticians but practitioners of his message. He invited them to identify with the sick, the lame, the poor, the untouchable, the unlovable, and the outcasts in society. Jesus' call was indeed a call of *kenosis*. It was a call to voluntarily renounce every comfort and privilege for the sake of others because Jesus emptied himself for others. The life of Jesus and his disciples is the archetype of the praxis of God's call.

Jesus' call reminds us today that his call is not to make monetary benefits and enlarge comfort zones. It does not entertain any personal demand for an easy life. There is no space for complaint in the call of Jesus. It does not motivate us to run after positions and power but engage with the lived realities of people. A genuine experience of God's call does not make a person a burden to God and others. Jesus calls a person to become a blessing and a beacon of hope to others. Jesus' call is not a call to fight and die for the offices and properties but to stand for the cause of love and justice. It is not a call to become an executive who carries out decisions of the councils or boards but live as a servant who hears the voice of Jesus and the people. The call of Jesus ultimately entails us maintaining its quality in faith, life, and ministry. The beauty of Jesus' call is that it comes to us with options: embrace or reject. There is no compulsion to embrace it. If a person is convinced of its worth, s/he can embrace it. But s/he has to pay the price for it: time, resources, energy, even life! If s/he does not have the courage or interest to accept Jesus' call, Jesus will not disrespect his/her decision. If one person does not respond, there is no shortage of people in the mission of God. If a person responds to Jesus' call affirmatively, there are consequences. S/he has to bear it.

Consequences

Every call has consequences. When a person is called for a job/ work, it involves pain, joy, and privileges. In the call of Jesus, suffering is an inevitable destiny. Dietrich Bonhoeffer very beautifully puts it, "when Jesus calls you, he calls you to come and die." It is not necessarily physical death or the end of life but surely an end (setting aside) of many desires, privileges, and comforts. It may lead to martyrdom which happened to the disciples of Jesus and even Bonhoeffer for listening to the voice of the Gospel of Jesus. The consequences of the call may come in different forms. It is not the experience of call but the ministry that comes out of it invites suffering. Commitment to call may inspire a person to decline an offer of a position or a seat of power. Jesus' call may not give him /her financial stability. S/he may not get the expected mobility and growth in life. There is no guarantee for comfort, respect, and acknowledgment in this world for embracing the call of Jesus. In the journey of experiencing a divine call, a person may encounter painful realities. S/he may have to imbibe pain for standing for the truth as Jesus stood as part of fulfilling His mission in this world. In the eyes of human beings, this pain may not be justifiable, but in God's sight, it is worth experiencing because it mediates divine favour to the people.

The joy of a called person is not material blessings s/he receives in this world but the liberated smile on the face of people with whom s/he works and the heavenly reward for his/her faithful response to the call of Jesus. For him/her, the privilege is primarily an experience of reproducing Christ and serving the people. S/he has transforming power than dominating power. As s/he embraces the call alone so s/he faces the consequences. But s/he has confidence that Jesus who called him/her is faithful to make his/her calling a blessing to others and pleasing to God. In the midst of challenging consequences, God gives strength to face them with a smiling face. S/he has to activate his/her calling under the shadow of God. Divine shadow is permanent, human shadow is temporary. S/he fails in his/her calling if s/he stands under the shadow of any human being (leader). A genuine call-consciousness resists him/her to become a devilish, selfish, chair-centered, pulpit-centered, leader-centered, money-centered 'servant.' But it takes him/her to the locations where Jesus waits for his faithful servants to touch the lives of people. Those who received the call of Jesus should live by the energy that comes from Jesus who came "not to be served but to serve, and to live life" for others. Jesus' call invites a person into the world of servants, who are ready to embody, the kenotic experience of Jesus.

27

Borderless Mission and God's Kingdom

There are many stories of vision in the Bible. They have multi-dimensional significance depending on how they are read today. The story of two visions and visionaries is recorded in Acts 10: 1-48. It narrates two visions, two actions, and two results. Cornelius and Peter had separate but interrelated visions and acted upon them. In the vision of Cornelius, an angel of God appeared and told him to send men to bring Peter to his house. Accordingly, Cornelius sent his men to Joppa where Peter stayed. The purpose and result of the vision is the salvation of Cornelius and his family as evident in the dialogue between Cornelius and Peter and the speech of Peter at Cornelius' house. While Cornelius' men were travelling to Joppa, Peter also had a vision of a large sheet containing animals, birds, and reptiles coming down from heaven. Then, he heard a voice asking him to kill and eat them. When he resisted eating, he heard a voice again telling him, "Do not call anything impure that God has made clean." After that, the sheet was taken back to heaven. Peter responded to Cornelius' request and visited his house. The entire story tells us that Peter's vision transformed his cultural mindset and prepared him to cross the borders of ethnicity and proclaim the Gospel to the Gentiles. This story presents a dialogue between two identities (Jew and Gentile), experiences, and visions. This dialogue begins with astonishment and cultural shock and ends with an outpouring of the Holy Spirit upon Gentiles and the beginning of a new faith journey with Jesus. Both Cornelius and Peter had gone through the process of transformation. Their story has missional significance in enlarging God's Kingdom on earth.

Break the Prejudices: A Step towards Borderless Mission and Kingdom Experience (vv 20 & 28)

An orthodox Jew always maintained socio-religious prejudices against non-Jews during the time of Jesus and his disciples. They believed that they were the only chosen people of God. They claimed racial superiority and treated others as inferior and impure. For them, a non-Jew was a Gentile. The religious and social outlook did not allow Jews to consider the Gentiles equal to them. For them, Gentiles had no revelatory experience of God. In this story, Cornelius is a Gentile, and Peter, a Jew. The initial response of Peter to the people, who gathered at Cornelius' house, shows that Peter was also influenced by the religious and racial pride of Jews. It means before the vision, he had a prejudice against the Gentiles. But the vision, he saw, had the power to break his prejudices against the Gentiles. After the vision, he was no longer a prisoner of prejudice but became a pioneer of a borderless mission. The vision exploded the myth that God did not care for the Gentiles. It proclaimed that Gentiles were also potential participants in God's Kingdom. God taught Peter that God does not discriminate against anyone, particularly those who are neglected and despised as 'no' people.

God always has a "preferential option" for them. When Jews were proud of their identity as God's people, God told them through the experience of Cornelius that Gentiles were also worthy of receiving God's favour and grace and becoming the people of God.

A prejudiced mind does not allow a person to connect with individuals who do not have a shared identity (caste/race), history, culture, and ethnicity. Many of us tend to associate with others based on their talents, qualifications, and social status. The prejudiced mind shapes their behavior and actions. While some are prisoners of a prejudiced mind, others are victims of a prejudiced mind. The latter are victims of the behavior of the former. The prejudiced mind defends binaries (pure-impure, superior-inferior) and perpetuates the culture of 'othering.' Through the story of Peter and Cornelius God says that He abhors a prejudiced mind. It is an impediment to the mission of God and the experience of God's Kingdom on this earth. God stands with the victims of prejudiced minds and assures them that they are also part of God's redemptive plan. A prejudiced mind kills the spirit of the Kingdom of God. God's Kingdom cannot be established on the pillars of prejudice. When we break the prejudices, the Kingdom of God emerges among us. When we break prejudices, the doors of borderless mission open to us. This happened in the life of Peter and Cornelius. When Peter broke the prejudices, Cornelius and his family experienced salvation, an experience of being part of God's Kingdom, which is yet to be consummated. Peter became a partner in God's mission to the Gentiles and an agent of God's Kingdom.

'Impure' in Social Relations but Pure in Borderless Mission and God's Kingdom (vv.14-16 & 28)

Through the vision, God tells Peter that he should not call anything impure. The implied view is that God has not created anything or anyone as impure or to be treated as impure. Pure-impure categorization is a human construct. God does not consider someone impure because of his/her color, caste, race, or gender. The so-called 'impure' is not actually 'impure' to God. Everyone is a potential being of purity and impurity. For God, every impurity/impure body can be purified. Pure-impure classification is also the product of a prejudiced mind. Peter had a vision in a cultural context that was shaped by the (Jewish) thinking that Gentiles were ritually impure because of their food habits, idolatry, lifestyle, etc. In the Indian context, the caste system also defined people in 'pure' and 'impure' categories based on their status in the caste hierarchy, occupation, and food habits. The Gentiles were defined as impure according to the social and religious laws of Jews. Peter's vision was a counter-narrative to the Jewish definition of Gentiles. The vision informed Peter that Gentiles might be impure for Jews but not for God. They are potential audiences of God's mission and participants in God's Kingdom.

The beauty of Peter's vision is that he had it when he was staying with Simon who was a tanner. Tanning was ritually defiling for Jews. It means, for an orthodox Jew, Peter had a vision at so-called 'impure house' owned by a so-called 'impure person' who was involved in the so-called 'impure' business. Probably, Simon was a Jew though he was involved in tanning work. Otherwise, Paul would not have said to the relatives of Cornelius that it was unlawful to associate with a Gentile and visit his house (v28). Perhaps, Simon was a Jewish Christian. No other Jew would give hospitality to a person like Peter." However, Peter had an unexpected vision in an unexpected location. Both the content and the location of the vision were radical.

There is no one impure in God's mission. God sent His son to save the so-called 'pure' and 'impure.' In God's kingdom, there is no pure-impure categorization. Both Jews and Gentiles are equal shareholders in the Kingdom of God. If we categorize people in terms of purity and impurity, we all are impure in one or another sense. A person may be ritually 'pure' but 'impure' in his/her approach, behavior, and thinking. Everyone needs the touch of God through a transforming vision as Peter had. S/he may be 'impure' in social and religious perceptions but not in the missional and the Kingdom framework. God's mission does not prevent anyone from inheriting the Kingdom of God.

Genuine Fellowship with God Breaks the Borders and Builds up the Kingdom of God

Human beings construct socio-cultural and religious borders with different purposes. Some justify such boundaries to protect the 'purity' of lineage and traditions. They use those borders to assert their hegemony over others also. The borders are built and sustained by cultural and social myths and prejudices. Human beings love to continue with the borders because they give him/her power, dominance, and privilege. They also wrongly think that borders give them security. Peter's vision informs us that God does not want the borders to continue in God's mission and Kingdom. God demolishes mental and physical borders by shaking the perceptions of people through radical visions. How did this happen to Peter? Genuine fellowship with God led Peter to a vision that taught him that he must break constructed borders that obstructed the mission of God and prevented the

Gentiles from being a part of the Kingdom inaugurated in Jesus. Divine fellowship transcends human borders and empowers a person to embrace everyone irrespective of social status. It opens the eyes of people and brings changes in their approach and relationships. God speaks the language of transformation to the people who are in genuine fellowship with God. If we are not able to break the boundaries, then our fellowship with God is not genuine. Divine fellowship compels us to act and break the boundaries and usher in God's Kingdom. When Peter broke the borders, God's mission began to flourish among the Gentiles. The Divine fellowship gives God's perspective to look at realities and build up God's Kingdom in this world.

Kingdom Belongs to God-fearing and Righteous People (vv. 34-35)

Peter realized that God does not show favoritism and accepts people who fear him and do what is right. Favoritism comes from a prejudiced mind. It is the 'quality' of people/communities with borders. Jews had religious and cultural justifications for favoritism. It comes out of their theological claim that they are the chosen people of God, and the law demands them to be separated from the Gentiles. For them, favouritism was not wrong from their theological perspective. They believed that they were righteous and God-fearing people because they followed the law of God. The vision of Peter tells us that the righteous cannot do favoritism. Those who fear God will do what is right (righteous) in the sight of God. God accepts anyone who fears God and lives a righteous life. This is God's way of favoritism. Salvation belongs to God-fearing and righteous people. They are inheritors of God's Kingdom. They are the real 'pure' people. When we do what is right in the sight of God, Kingdom appears amongst us.

Peter obeyed the vision, crossed the boundaries, and straightened the unequal social relationship. When a Jew visited the house of a Gentile, people not only heard the Gospel of Jesus but also experienced the dawn of God's Kingdom among them. Their stigma of Gentile identity was removed by the outpouring of the Holy Spirit. This was an experience of God's Kingdom. They were no longer inferior beings but empowered by the Spirit to witness Christ. Peter's engagement with the Gentiles explains the goal of the Christian mission today: making people God-fearing and righteous by faith and action. To achieve this goal, we should cross borders and engage with people longing to begin a new journey.

Be an Agent of Transforming Vision and Mission

The story of the dialogue of two visions, particularly the experience of Peter points to the significance of a transforming vision and mission. People may have visions, but it does not necessarily lead to the transformation of an individual or a community. Peter had a vision that changed his mentality about Gentiles and his understanding of the mission. It transformed his perspective and led him to an experience of conversion. He crossed the walls of a 'prejudiced mind' and embraced the so-called 'impure' people. It is a sign of conversion. He was not simply seeing the vision but became an agent of the mission that actualizes the vision. The vision empowered him to take bold steps to get into a 'stigmatized' terrain. His visit, speech, and gesture gave hope to the Gentiles. It was an experience of empowerment for them. Thus, he also became an agent of empowerment. Today, we should expect from God a bold vision that transforms us and leads us into locations that people have not yet ventured into. We should receive a borderless vision for a borderless mission. A borderless transforming vision enables a person to cross the boundaries to touch the people, who are rejected and despised, and to build up the Kingdom of God among them. There are no human borders for a mission, and no boundary can be fixed for God's Kingdom. God invites everyone to God's Kingdom through borderless transforming vision and mission.

28

New Beginning

Human beings make decisions about a 'new beginning' in different stages of life. It may be related to personal, family, or professional life. When they land in a crisis or are caught for wrong decisions/actions, human beings resolve to begin afresh. It may be partially or fully successful in life. Sometimes, an individual relapses into the 'past' life. Christianity teaches us that a new life begins with Jesus and sustains through Him. The Bible talks about a story of a woman (John 8: 1-11) who experienced the process of a new beginning at the feet of Jesus. According to the story, the Scribes and Pharisees brought a woman, caught in adultery, to Jesus when he was teaching in the temple. They asked Jesus "What do you say?" about her action as the Law of Moses commanded that she should be stoned to death. They raised this question intending to accuse him if he would disagree with the Mosaic Law. They might have thought that Jesus would challenge the law because of his liberal and compassionate outlook. Contrary to the expectation of Scribes and Pharisees, Jesus gave a wonderful judgment. He neither nullified the law nor punished the woman. He told her, "Go and sin no more." That was a new beginning in her life. Jesus' judgment was a sound theological judgment that affirmed her life. It was not a judgment that incarcerated her life but set her free for a new beginning.

In this story, Jesus protected the life of a woman in a Jewish social context shaped by patriarchal prejudices and injunctions against women. She was a victim of archaic patriarchal law that demanded the adulteress be stoned to death. She was looked down upon as an object of pleasure than a person. In Jewish thinking, she was born to be a 'helper' to man. As a woman, she was ritually impure, intellectually inferior, physically weak, and poor in decision-making. She was not equal to man. Her witness had no validity in the judicial system. She was not counted in Jewish religious life. If Jesus had followed the law as expected by the patriarchal mind of the time, she would have been buried in the grave of patriarchy. This story gives some lessons to facilitate the process of a new beginning in human life, particularly in the lives of others.

Accusation: An Instrument of Destruction, Not Construction (vv 4-6)

When the scribes and Pharisees accused the woman caught in adultery and demanded punishment, Jesus "stooped down and wrote on the ground with his finger, as though he did not hear." The body language of Jesus shows that he was not interested in the accusations that destroyed human life. He did not pay attention to the accusations of self-righteous scribes and Pharisees. The Bible does not say what he wrote on the ground. His gesture was not completely ignoring the allegation but the destructive intention behind it. He understood that this accusation was not going to construct but kill her. He knew her state of mind and the self-righteous consciousness of the accusers, the Pharisees. She must be emotionally and physically shattered. Every word and action of the accusers must have pierced her heart and disturbed her psyche. Perhaps, she was going through the last minutes of her life in this world. In that dreadful situation, Jesus' silence and body language must have given her hope for life. Jesus accused neither the woman nor the people because he knew that accusation would not construct a person. Jesus intended to construct the life of both the accuser and the accused. For him, the conversion of the accuser and the accused was equally important for the Kingdom of God. In this story, Jesus teaches us that accusation destroys people, particularly their prospects. It does not facilitate a new beginning in his/her life. In our daily life, we accuse others for no reason. For many, it has become part of their lives. They are ignorant that their approach does not build up a person. A follower of Jesus is called to construct the lives of people. Jesus, who knows the mind of the accused and the accuser, is the best judge. However, Jesus' approach does not encourage complacency. He does not tell that a person does not need to attend or listen to the accusations because some allegations may not be unfounded. Jesus protects a person from destruction but s/he should not give space for others to accuse him/her. It calls for him/her to become more responsible in personal, family, and professional life.

New Method of Judgment (v 7)

The question of scribes and Pharisees did not elicit an immediate response from Jesus. When they continued to ask him, Jesus responded, "He who is without sin among you, let him throw a stone at her first." They might have expected that Jesus would have either allowed them to stone her or invalidate the law. For them, either of the options would have served their purpose: implement the law or accuse Jesus as a violator of the law. Jesus redefined the method of judgment. Normally the history or the character of the complainant/accuser may not be considered to judge a case. The merit and the evidence/ witness of the offence determine the judgment. But Jesus asked the accusers to prove their credibility to demand punishment against this woman. At the same time, Jesus did not say that she was right. This approach had an equal effect on the accusers and the accused. While it exposed the self-righteousness of the accusers, it did not approve of the sin of the accused. For Jesus, the sinner (self-righteous person) has no moral right to judge or punish a person. Therefore, before judging others, a Christian should ask the question; does s/he have the moral right to point a finger against someone? If s/he genuinely asks the question, s/he may have to put the stones down on most occasions. Jesus advises that we should judge ourselves first. It means we should throw stones at ourselves first, then that stone should hit others. The stone should hit our pride, criticism, judging nature, and inactiveness. Jesus' method transforms both the accuser and the accused. It reduces the number of times a person aims stones at others. This method does not condone the sinful life but gives a chance to begin a new life. It underlines that human beings cannot become perfect judges because of their fallen nature. Their biased framework does not build up a person. God is the ultimate judge. God knows the motives and the inner state of every person in the accuser-accused relationship.

Genuine Introspection: A Hallmark of Christian Identity (vv 9)

Jesus' response had an immediate reaction from the scribes and Pharisees. It was not a verbal reaction but a physical action. According to the narrative, they did not counter Jesus with their arguments. The people, who came to stone this woman, left the place without stoning her. They came with the support of the law. But their argument could not stand before the words of

Jesus. The physical disappearance of the accusers corresponds to the defeat of their legalistic theology. Despite their negative intentions and legalistic approach, the scribes and the Pharisees remind us of the virtue of genuine introspection. They could have still stoned the woman and pretended to be righteous. But they had gone through the process of genuine introspection. Their action points to two things. Firstly, everyone can start afresh. In this case, we cannot negate that at least some of them must have come out of their primitive thinking about women and their interpretation of the law. Second, Jesus' words have the power to lead anyone into the realm of introspection if s/he has a genuine encounter with Jesus. One cannot resist genuine introspection in the presence of Jesus. For me, they are the prototype for Christians today. If this event happens today, many Christians will throw stones at her. The level of dishonesty is very high among many Christians. They cover up their unrighteous mind through 'self-righteous' actions. Their actions may not really speak their minds. The scribes and Pharisees manifested their integrity though they were self-righteous till they encountered Jesus. When we look inside, we understand our weaknesses and ineligibility to judge others. It helps us correct and move forward with a new approach. A Christian must be known for his/her virtue of introspection in action, not for throwing stones at others. S/he is a builder of lives. S/he does not carry stones, but seeds of love, compassion, and hope.

Beyond Punishment (v 10-11)

The law demands punishment for unlawful actions. The woman was brought to Jesus with the intention to punish her. If they had not brought her to Jesus, they would not have had any obstacles to killing her. Indeed, their strategy backfired. Jesus teaches that there is a stage of correction beyond punishment.

It is a stage of repentance. It is a stage of hope and comfort. In other words, it is a stage of a second chance. This stage should be explored before punishment. Punishment is not the final destiny. It may satisfy the custodians of the law but may not always help a person evolve into his/her full potential. Jesus does not reject punishment altogether. But he questions a punishment that destroys a person. He rejects legalism that does not give a chance to improve. In this story, the Pharisees wanted to kill her without giving her any chance to make corrections in her life. For Jesus, there is always a scope for correction in everyone's life. There is no situation outside the realm of rectification. There is always room for improvement, refinement, and growth in human life. It is easy to punish people but difficult to bring a person to repentance. While human law is blind to life, Jesus' law embraces life and protects it from death. Jesus' law of love gives a chance not to continue in sin but to start a new life. While the law empowers its custodians to even take life, Jesus gives life to people and enables them to celebrate life in its fullness. Today, the law is not bad in democratic societies, but how it is read to address human issues do matter. It can be misused to curtail freedom and destroy people's lives just as the Pharisees did with the woman. People think within the framework of law and punishment. Jesus encourages them to think and act through the frame of protecting life. It means we need to think beyond punishment.

Jesus' Judgment: A Judgment of Life Affirmation (v. 11)

The most powerful statement in this story is "Neither do I condemn you; go and sin no more." The scribes and Pharisees had already judged her before bringing her to Jesus. They judged her based on the law. They just delayed the execution of the judgment to know the opinion of Jesus in this case. Jesus pronounced a wonderful judgment though he was not the 'judge' in the episode. The accusers had to reverse their judgment after hearing Jesus' response, "He who is without sin among you, may throw a stone at her first." In effect, they could not condemn her. Now, Jesus also says, "Neither do I condemn you..." He did not give her license to continue in her sinful life. He told her, "Go and sin no more." At the beginning of the event, she was seen only as an object, an object of sex, and then became a subject of debate. But Jesus treated her with gentleness and compassion. For Jesus, she was a person, a child of God, not a sinner who could not be redeemed. His words of life gave her identity back. She is no longer a person carrying the stigma of adultery. She is not an object of contempt but a person with a new beginning. Jesus' judgment was a judgment of life because it gave her a life that the law would have destroyed. His judgment does not lead people to death but to life. The words of Jesus have the power to transform a person and empower him/her to resist the temptations of sin. The internalization of his words generates power within a person to detach from a sinful past, accusing nature, and judgmental behavior. As Jesus affirmed life in his judgment, a follower of Jesus should affirm life in his/her words or actions of judgment. It should lead a person to repentance and renewal.

New Beginning: An Outcome of Encounter with Jesus

The woman's ordeal began with her being caught by the scribes and Pharisees for adultery. She would never have thought that she would be alive. Probably, she might not have known that they would take her to Jesus. She also would not have thought that she would get protection from Jesus. Perhaps, she was unaware that Jesus came to save sinners. Until she came face to face with Jesus, she was a sinner. At the end of the story, she became a person ready to chart a new journey in life. Jesus changed her life neither by punishing nor accusing her but by offering his grace and compassionate presence. His presence protected her from death and directed her to a new path of forgiveness, love, and mercy. Her encounter with Jesus was not an experience of confrontation or interrogation but of assuring life. The repentance happened not only in her life but also in the lives of the Pharisees. None dared to throw stones at her. Those who came to execute Mosaic Law went away by learning a new lesson from Jesus. They were also shown the way of love and forgiveness. They also must have decided to begin afresh in life. Whoever encountered Jesus with an open mind has been transformed. A new beginning is an outcome of an encounter with Jesus. This story encourages us to encounter Jesus for a new direction in life, perspective, and action. The change in one person can contribute to the change in many people. Life becomes meaningful if it is subject to renewal and searches for a new beginning.

29

Gethsemane:
A Journey from Crisis to Courage

The episode in Gethsemane (Matthew 26: 36-56) is the starting point of Jesus' journey toward the Cross. It happens after Jesus' last supper with his disciples. According to the narrative, Jesus came with his disciples to a place called Gethsemane, known for a garden, and asked them to pray. He felt extremely sorrowful within himself. But his disciples failed to stay with him in prayer. He was much distressed and even prayed that "O My Father, if it is possible, let this cup pass from me; nevertheless, not as I will, but as you will." Jesus' arrest and Judas' betrayal also happened in this garden. There are different opinions regarding the exact location of this garden. However, it is believed that this garden was located on the western side of the Mount of Olives in Jerusalem. Today, it is a pilgrim site. It has a story to tell, a story of journey from Crisis to Courage in Jesus' life.

Gethsemane is not simply a garden or a geographical location. It is a journey. It symbolically summarizes the Christian journey that starts from a crisis to a point where we courageously embrace Christ and walk with him on the rough pathway of life. Jesus' experience at Gethsemane gives us insights that may empower our Christian journey.

Gethsemane: Location of Agony, Prayer (Divine Encounter) and Courage (vv. 36, 38 & 46)

People visit gardens for different purposes: enjoying time with friends and family, relaxation, social gatherings, holiday parties, or refreshing minds, etc. Many might have visited the garden of Gethsemane on the day of Jesus' arrest. For them, it could have been a place of relaxation, delight, or fun. Perhaps, his disciples also visited the garden with different expectations. But Jesus had a different experience in the garden, which even his disciples could not understand. For him, it was a place of agony, prayer, and courage. He experienced excruciating pain within. He did not explain it in detail to his disciples but requested them to pray. Probably, he might not have gone through such moments of agony during his ministry. The story informs us that the garden where he endured pain was also a location of divine encounter. Amid agony, he had a divine encounter in which he became courageous to face an impending challenge. Through divine encounter, the agonized self became a courageous self. The location of agony is a site of internalizing faith. Symbolically, this location may be a crisis in life, an experience of exclusion, negation or disease, or rejection today. The location of agony does not remain the same in human life. Jesus' experience underlines that it may transform into a location of divine encounter and courage. The garden of Gethsemane symbolizes a journey from a location of agony to a location of divine encounter and courage. It is also a redemptive experience.

Prayer: Protective Shield against Temptation (v. 41)

In this episode, Jesus asked his disciples to pray so that they might not fall into temptation. It could be a temptation of disciples not to pray or a possible reckless reaction of disciples to Judas' betrayal and Roman soldiers and disrupt God's plan of human salvation. It also could be a temptation of Jesus to go away from God's will in his life. Sometimes, human beings come to the point where they will be tempted to act contrary to their beliefs and values or run away from God's will. At the moment of temptation, prayer functions as a protective shield. Jesus prayed so that he and his disciples might not be tempted at the crucial moment of his life and mission. It reminds us that temptation is a part of the Christian journey. Prayer helps us overcome temptations. It also helps us discern the will of God as we stand at the crossroads of life. God does not will His people to be ensnared by temptation. It depends on how we respond to God's will. For a Christian, constant prayer is the shield because it provides energy to face any temptation.

Finite nature of Human Fellowship and Infinite Nature of Divine Fellowship (vv. 38-40, 43)

This storyline depicts Jesus' experience of loneliness at the decisive moment of his mission in this world. He asked his disciples to pray for strength to overcome the agony he had gone through. When he saw that his disciples could not stay with him in prayer, he must have felt lonely. In human life, loneliness becomes acute when we feel that friends, who know us closely, fail to understand our pain and accompany us to sail through the currents of agony. Jesus' experience of loneliness points to the fact that human fellowship is temporary, but a divine fellowship is permanent. The former is fragile, and the latter is everlasting. Human fellowship always exhibits its finite nature because it is conditioned by contextual human needs and emotions. Human beings have physical, cognitive, and spiritual limitations that restrict them to identify with fellow beings. Loneliness is not simply physical. We experience it when others do not understand our mind, ideas, language, perspective, etc. Though they were sleeping, the disciples were 'physically' present to protect Jesus. However, they could not understand Jesus' agonized mind and his language of pain. The disciples slept when Jesus needed them the most. Here Jesus' experience tells us that others may sleep, but God does not sleep when we walk through the valley of loneliness. Loneliness does not have the power to stop us from our destiny if we have the consciousness that divine fellowship has infinite power. We need to move forward with the assurance that God is with us. We have not come to this world alone. God walks with us as a permanent companion in this world.

Boldness in the midst of Crisis (v. 39 & 42)

Jesus prayed to his Father to remove the cup of agony that leads to the consummating moment of his mission. It is quite natural for Christ in human form to offer such a prayer. However, he did not insist on relief from the crisis but surrendered his will to God's will. He boldly uttered that God's will is his will. This is the actual point of divine encounter in which a person acknowledges the sovereignty and the plan of God in his/her life. Jesus was willing to endure the consequences of accepting God's will. Christian faith teaches that God's will alone prevails over human will. Following the pattern of Jesus' prayer, Christians seek God's will in every aspect of their lives. It can also be said that a Christian is one who proclaims that his/her will is God's will, which is ultimately manifested in Jesus' life and teachings. The internalization of the will of God gives the courage to face the crisis. On the one hand, Jesus and his teachings make a person courageous to embrace God's will. On the other hand, one needs boldness to seek God's will amid crises. Jesus is the model of being courageous at times of crisis. God's will is prophetic, missional, and purposive.

Agony: Entry point of Gethsemane; Courage: Exit point (vv. 38, 45-46)

Jesus entered the garden with agony that anybody who accompanied him could hardly understand. He bore it within himself and mustered the courage to face it. Symbolically, for Jesus, the agony was the entry point of Gethsemane. He did not remain in agony without any solution. He came out of the garden with a solution. The answer to his prayer was not a complete relief from the agony that he would have expected. Gethsemane has a different view of the solution to a crisis: courage. It means Jesus' experience redefined the concept of a solution to a crisis in human life. Jesus at Gethsemane invites us to courageously face the crisis without which it will not be solved. This is the will of God. God does not expect us to run away from the agony because 'facing' it has the power to prepare us for attaining a greater purpose in life. Jesus faced the agony so that he could prepare himself for the impending pain on the cross. That pain conquered the power of sin and accomplished salvation for humanity. Gethsemane prepared Jesus for Calvary. When Roman soldiers came to arrest him, Jesus had already exited his 'Gethsemane.' He did not resist the arrest but went with them to face the trial. He was not timid and emotional but courageous to embrace God's will. Jesus' experience at Gethsemane defines Christian life not as an experience of escape from a crisis/problem but as a testimony of facing it and being prepared to accept God's will.

Personal Gethsemane

Every human being has a personal Gethsemane. As mentioned earlier, it can be an experience of loneliness, injustice, discrimination, disease, etc. Personal Gethsemane shapes our thinking, purifies our mind, renews the human spirit, deconstructs our perceptions, and locates us in God's will. A Christian without Gethsemane experience does not mature in faith. Gethsemane is the test of Christian maturity: whether s/he surrenders to God's will. S/he learns to listen to God at Gethsemane. S/he hears a small but courageous voice from God in the personal garden of Gethsemane. The beauty of Gethsemane experience is that s/he proclaims that "…I no longer live but Christ lives in me" (Galatians 2:20). This is the time we realize God's will and develop productive prayer life/relationship with God and receive the courage to face any challenge. The distance between crisis and courage may appear to be long in the personal garden of Gethsemane. God can reduce it by strengthening us to face the crisis. Jesus bridges the two poles in life: Crisis and Courage. Personal Gethsemane starts with a crisis but ends with courage. Gethsemane is the story of a Christian journey!

30

The Cross

Every religion has symbols that communicate the faith of its adherents. The cross is the most revered symbol in Christianity. It not only symbolizes an event but also contains the essence of Christian faith. As a symbol, it points to and embodies reality. The sacrificial death of Jesus Christ and cosmic salvation is the reality imbibed on the cross. The cross may evoke different feelings in the minds of people subject to their context, need and perspective. They celebrate the event of the cross by appropriating the symbol in different ways (revering, worshiping and considering it as source of motivation) and by applying its meaning in their lives. The energy that flows from the cross empowers the weak, transforms the self-righteous, strengthens the vulnerable, leads the sinner to repentance and assures him/her eternal life. The cross is not an object to be admired but an experience of identifying with Christ to partake in the mission of God in this world. Salvation breaks out when people experience the cross.

Cross: Starting Point of New Life in Christ

The cross defines the relationship between God and human beings. It heals the estrangement and restores the right relationship between the divine and the human. Therefore, the outcome of the cross must be 'the end of sinful life and beginning of righteous life.' That is why Peter says (1 Peter 2:24) "He himself bore our sins....we might die to sins and live for righteousness..." The biblical righteousness calls for a 'right relationship' with God and fellow beings. The efficacy of the cross depends upon how one responds to the cross by establishing and maintaining the right relationship with God and fellow beings. When we attempt to heal the wounds of brokenness with others, the new life in Christ begins to flow from the cross. The experience of new life in Christ is a proof of the power of the cross in personal and community life. The power of the cross manifests where people attempt to establish the right relationship. Those who preserve the right relationship only can say as Paul said, "....It is no longer I who live, but Christ who lives..." (Gal 2:20) Jesus, through his death on the cross, inaugurated a new life of right relationship among human beings. It is the responsibility of believers to take the new life in its fullness. The cross becomes meaningless to the people who are least concerned to develop the right relationship with God and fellow human beings. The right relationship with God naturally reflects in the mutual relationship of human beings. The rituals may not help them establish the right relationship. But they can point to the need of living in the right relationship with God and human beings.

A new life in Christ is not only individualistic but a communitarian experience also. Therefore, we should develop the right relationship within the family, church, society, workplace, ministry locations etc. The cross appears brightly where the right relationship exists. The right relationship has redemptive value because it determines the salvation of individuals. Hence, it is also the starting point of the ultimate salvation anticipated in the future. It requires the believers to become vehicles of redemption for themselves and others through building up the right relationship.

Cross: Symbol of the Eruption of Hope for Humanity

Traditionally, the cross is understood as a symbol of suffering, pain etc. However, its symbolism goes beyond traditional thinking and interpretations. In fact, the cross is the dynamic symbol of hope. It symbolizes hope in the midst of anguish, despair, helplessness, rejection, God-forsakenness, etc. The cross teaches that Jesus' life on the cross did not end without resurrection in this world. Though he experienced God-forsakenness momentarily Jesus did not lose his hope in God in the midst of extreme agony. He surrendered himself to God's will that is salvific, liberative and hopeful. Indeed, the cross finally declared him Christ for every human being. Therefore, the cross inspires us to see hope manifest in it. It is not pain or suffering alone that comes out from the cross, but the rays of hope for the entire humanity. It loudly proclaims that 'you have a hope to live with.' It is a hope of new life in its fullness in this world and the world to come. As lava comes out of a volcano, the hope strongly but gently erupts from the cross. S/he can internalize the hope from the cross and boldly face any challenges that the world throws into his/her life. A Christian who claims the 'sentimental ownership' of the cross must re-examine his/her faith-life that whether the cross continues to remain as a symbol of hope for him or her. If s/he goes through a critical situation in life and says that "I am carrying a cross now" then s/he fails to tap the power of hope in the cross. It is a pessimistic statement that comes out of despair and anxiety. But s/he who imbibes the hope that erupts from the cross of Jesus optimistically deals with the challenges in life. If the cross does not become a symbol of hope, s/he cannot experience redemption in personal and community life. The cross as the symbol of hope must motivate people to fight against odd realities in life. Redemption in everyday life means actualizing hope in the midst of broken realities.

Cross: Our Pride

Since the cross stands as the symbol of new life and hope that the world does not give us, we must boast in the cross (Gal 6:14). Christians can boast for their lives today because of the cross planted in Calvary. The cross has given them new life in sinful and lifeless conditions. It also has given them hope in the midst of hopelessness. It is the cross that has taught them how to face the challenges in life. It is the cross that has facilitated their redemption from the bondage of sin. It is the cross that continually reminds them to cultivate the right relationship for experiencing God's Kingdom in their midst. On the cross, God defeated the life-negating forces forever. Therefore, the cross should not remain an object of adoration or decoration. S/he should boast in the cross by releasing its power (practically experiencing new life and hope) in individual and community life. It brings transformation to the sinful world. Boasting in the cross should not be limited to proclamation alone. It calls for praxis in every realm of life. If s/he boasts in the cross, he/she must carry the cross in lifestyle. The cross that Jesus carried was for the redemption of entire humanity. If s/he does boast in the cross, s/he must first become the channel of redemption to those who are in tears, loss, crisis, and under the bondage of the powers and principalities of this world.

31

The Last Words on the Cross

Jesus made seven statements on the cross. They can be called the Last Words of Jesus on the cross. Every year Christians remember and reflect on these statements (sayings) during Good Friday service in church. They believe that Jesus was crucified on Friday and his last words have redemptive and ethical value in the salvation experience. These words are important because he uttered them in the last stage of his redemptive mission in this world. Christians revere these words because they came out of the pain that He endured for the salvation of humanity. As the words have historical and contemporary significance so the day also gets its due meaning in the minds of believers.

What is *good* in 'Good Friday?' Traditionally Christians believe that this is the day Lord Jesus Christ died for the remission of their sins. In my language, Malayalam, 'Good Friday' is called *dhukka velli,* which means 'Sad Friday' though 'good' in Good Friday linguistically does not imply 'sad.' The 'good' cannot be 'sad.' This Friday is called 'Good Friday' because it is the day that brought something 'Good' to the entire creation. It is on this day, God achieved something highest good for the creation. The highest good is the salvation of entire creation from the power of sin originated from the disobedience of Adam and Eve. It came to humanity through the death of Jesus on the cross. The power that flows from the cross enables us to experience the 'good' achieved by God through Jesus Christ. For Christians, this day is the day of great joy because this day facilitated/assured our eternal life. By faith, we receive salvation through Jesus' death. It is not the Friday that generated sorrow but happiness. The words that Jesus uttered on the cross (Last Words) have implications for Christian life today.

Jesus: Embodiment of Forgiveness

Jesus said, "Father, forgive them, for they do not know what they are doing." (Luke 23:34)

According to the Gospel of Luke, Jesus was crucified along with two criminals. "Father, forgive them, for they do not know what they are doing." This is the first statement of Jesus on the cross. In this statement, Jesus requests his Father to forgive those who executed his crucifixion. They are apparently Jewish religious authorities and fundamentalists, and the Roman ruling class including the soldiers. The statement points to the virtue of forgiveness, one of the constituent elements of Jesus' life and mission. Therefore, it also makes up one of the ingredients of the Christian faith. This statement is the practical culmination of Jesus' teaching and ministry of forgiveness. He became an embodiment of forgiveness on the cross.

Cross: The Symbol of Ultimate Forgiveness

Luke 23: 34 records one of the most powerful sayings of Jesus Christ. It embodies the crux of the Christian faith and its praxis. The Christian faith is the faith of forgiveness. It teaches us the value of forgiveness and mandates its adherents to forgive one another. Its *kerygma* explains the power of forgiveness ultimately manifested in the cross of Jesus Christ. The message of divine forgiveness has attracted many to Christianity throughout the centuries. On the cross, Jesus showed the need and beauty of forgiveness. On the cross, we witness the celebration of divine forgiveness. This forgiveness ended the historical alienation of humanity from God. In his ministry, Jesus taught the message of unconditional forgiveness for everyone irrespective of creed, color or caste. It has no borders and custodians and is accessible to anyone who approaches Jesus. He revealed and practiced forgiveness that is eternal in scope. It facilitates people to experience eternal life offered through His death on the cross. In the economy of salvation, the cross of Jesus stands as a symbol of ultimate forgiveness. While the cross has symbolic power to evoke our consciousness, his death offers ultimate forgiveness that guarantees eternal life.

Jesus asked his Father to forgive his persecutors at the moment of highest pain. He pleaded for their forgiveness because they were ignorant of what they were doing with him. This moment was the finale of what he taught and practiced during his earthly ministry. He embodied the profundity of forgiveness and presented himself as a model to be emulated by his disciples. The symbol of the cross today invites us to participate in the embodiment of forgiveness in family, faith communities and larger society. It confronts us to forgive others who have knowingly and unknowingly wronged us. The cross becomes meaningful through the experiences of forgiveness. It is a liberating and gratifying experience for the forgiver and the one who is forgiven. The cross of Jesus not only points to a historical event but also creates a present event of forgiveness.

No Forgiveness without Pain

Jesus forgave his executioners when he was enduring the pain on the cross. It happened at the time of highest pain he might have experienced in his life. The forgiveness that follows from the cross originates from the pain of Jesus. It teaches that God's plan of salvation involves pain. Divine justice required the punishment of human sin. But Jesus stood on behalf of us and experienced the pain of punishment that was due for humanity and met the divine requirement to forgive us. There is no eternal forgiveness without pain. God felt pain when God's Son endured the pain for channelizing forgiveness to human beings. It means divine forgiveness is costly but worthy. The forgiver experiences more pain than the forgiven person who may experience pain out of his/her guilty consciousness. The followers of Jesus are beneficiaries of divine forgiveness that came to them through the pain of Jesus.

The forgiveness that Jesus manifested on the cross is a signpost for mutual forgiveness among human beings. It is not easy to forgive another person because genuine forgiveness demands the forgiver to walk an extra mile and give up his/her ego and mind of vengeance and forget what s/he experienced in the past. It is more painful when s/he remembers the pain, loss or humiliation inflicted in the past and unconditionally forgives the perpetrator and embraces him/her into the fellowship. Though the process is painful the strength to go through the process comes from Jesus who willingly experienced deep pain to get forgiveness for us. When we forgive others, we cannot do it without pain. But the beauty of experiencing this pain is that it gives life to others. As divine forgiveness saved humanity from the punishment of sin, so mutual forgiveness saves the victim and the victimizer from the consciousness of revenge and guilt respectively. It enriches this worldly life that is destined for eternity. A Christian lives by forgiveness and with a mind of forgiveness and for the community of forgiveness.

No Future without Forgiveness

There is a future aspect of forgiveness. Archbishop Desmond Tutu wrote a book entitled *No Future without Forgiveness*. Though he has written the book in the context of South Africa, the title of the book helps us understand the future aspect of forgiveness (impact of forgiveness) that was manifested on the cross. God realized that the future of sinful human beings depended on divine forgiveness. Without divine forgiveness, they would have been condemned to death. Their future, salvation, was impossible without divine forgiveness because they sinned against God. Jesus bought this forgiveness for humanity through his death on the cross. The broken relationship between God and human beings were restored through forgiveness. It also means forgiveness of God determined the future relationship between God and human beings. Jesus' ministry and his death on the cross proved that forgiveness is the weapon of the strong, not the weak. It is divine in essence and eternal in purpose.

As the relationship between God and human beings could not grow without forgiveness, so no community can grow without experiencing forgiveness in social/familial relations. Both the forgiver and the forgiven are healed by the act of forgiveness. It leads to building up a new community. Forgiveness decides the future of an individual, faith community, society and nation. It opens new horizons of relationships, celebration, sharing and mutuality. Christian community is a new community, born out of divine forgiveness. It has to continue as a beacon of forgiveness that contributes to the transformation of this world. The forgiveness that Jesus gave on the cross is the representative gesture for the forgiveness of human sins done against God and human beings. Jesus, the embodiment of forgiveness, calls for every human being to forgive one another to build up new communities of forgiveness in respective contexts. The mind of forgiveness is divine, but the mind of retribution is profane.

Jesus: Assurance of Eternal Life (Salvation)

"I tell you the truth, today you will be with me in paradise." (Luke 23:43)

While on the cross, Jesus saw the soldiers who divided his clothes, the public who mocked him with humiliating comments and the criminals who argued on his painful condition. One of the criminals, who were crucified with him, threw an insulting question to Jesus, "Aren't you the Christ? Save yourself and us!" But the other criminal reprimanded him and said, "We are punished justly, for we are getting what our deeds deserve, but this man has done nothing wrong." He also said, "Jesus, remember me when you come into your kingdom." To his request, Jesus uttered his second statement on the cross.

Introspection: The First Step to Salvation

The conversation shows that the criminal knew why he was crucified. His introspective mind did not allow him to justify his past and denounce the punishment he deserved. While accepting the punishment, he hoped for a new life through Jesus. He did not limit his introspective mind to evaluate his condition on the cross alone but boldly looked at the injustice done to Jesus. He realized that Jesus was unjustly crucified. This is why he said Jesus did not do any wrong. Probably, he knew Jesus and his ministry before the crucifixion. Otherwise, he would not have said, "Jesus, remember me when you come into your kingdom." (v 42) The introspection happened when he encountered Jesus on the cross. It led him to eternal life as Jesus assured. Though Jesus and the criminal might have experienced the same amount of pain the former was the source of salvation and the latter the source of introspection. The criminal realized not only his sinful past but also what Christ could do for him at present and in the future. For him, Jesus embodied the assurance of eternal life and continues to assure the same for generations.

He did not ask Jesus to perform a miracle as demanded by another criminal. He pleaded Jesus to remember him in his kingdom. It means he opted for eternal life than temporary relief from the cross. Perhaps, he must have heard about eternal life taught by Jesus Christ. Put it differently, there was no chance for him to be released from the cross. But there was a chance for him to be released from eternal condemnation. He used the opportunity to get an assurance of eternal life from Jesus. The introspective and repentant consciousness of the criminal convinced Jesus to accept him into the kingdom. The criminal must have also believed that Jesus could exonerate him from his past transgressions. In the presence of Jesus, nobody can hide his/her transgressions. Two options are available for those who encounter Jesus: either confess the sins and receive salvation or cover up the sins within himself/herself (not possible before Jesus) and before the public and live a life without assurance of salvation. The introspective mind that allows the genuine encounter with Jesus accepts the mistakes and seeks the remission of sins and gets into the track of salvation offered in Jesus Christ. It facilitates to begin a new life in this world and continue it in the world to come promised by Jesus Christ. For Jesus, everyone is a potential recipient of eternal life provided s/he needs to have an introspective and repentant mind.

Remember me in your Kingdom: Bold Request

Instead of asking for an instant escape from the cross, the criminal with an introspective and repentant mind requested him something different from other requests Jesus heard before. In the moment of unbearable pain, he made a 'strange request' from a human point of view. His request would have surprised Jesus too! In his ministry, Jesus encountered many requests for healing from diseases, deliverance from demonic possession, life from death etc. Here a criminal made a bold request to enter the kingdom of Jesus. For me, it is bold because he asked it in an odd situation but with the hope of accomplishing it. This request involved confession and hope. His request implied that Jesus would establish his kingdom even though he was hung on the cross now. It shows the strong faith that he developed within few hours of his direct encounter with Jesus. He might have been confident that Jesus would not turn down his request. His bold request came out of his bold confidence in Jesus.

When he encountered Jesus on the cross the criminal got the courage to request him eternal life (life in the kingdom). Jesus always opened the space for others to make their requests to him. He never ran away from them. He lived with the people and died along with the people (the criminals). Therefore, they could directly request him of their physical and spiritual needs. His life with the people also gave him opportunities to hear the requests that came out of their painful realities. Amazingly, he heard the request of a person at the point of his death. The pain on the cross did not deter him from listening to the request of his 'companion' at the time of the crucifixion. In his response to the criminal, Jesus set a model for human beings to become humane to the requests of fellow beings who approach with their pain and hope. Only the broken people make bold requests.

Bold requests open the mind of God and get the assurance of life in this world and the Kingdom of God. Jesus' statement on the cross gives assurance of granting the requests made out of brokenness, forsakenness and helplessness.

Genuine Confession leads to New Life/New Status in Jesus

The criminal was genuine in his confession and request on the cross. He made the request not to prove his ideological attachment to Jesus or to empathize with him but to save his life from eternal condemnation. He confessed that he was a criminal. But his encounter with Jesus enabled him to have a new look at his life. He knew that he would die in this world but Jesus assured him that he would not die forever. "…Today you will be with me in paradise" came an unexpected life-changing declaration to the genuine confession of the criminal. The expression 'today' shows an immediate effect on the assurance of Jesus. He did not expect relief from the cross to live a life in this world, but he got relief from it to celebrate eternal life with Jesus. If he was not genuine Jesus would not have promised him life in paradise. Whoever confronted Jesus genuinely they were transformed to experience a new beginning in life.

The beauty of this saying is that amid pain Jesus was concerned about the salvation of human beings. He came to this world to save humanity from the power of sin. His mission invited people to receive the gift of salvation. Jesus' promise of eternal life to the criminal is the sign of his promise to all who confess their sins and believe in Jesus. The criminal who responded to Jesus on the cross became a new person qualified to enter the Kingdom of God. He received new status through the assurance of Jesus. He was no more a criminal but a member of God's kingdom. His short journey with Jesus began with introspection and confession. In that journey, he made a bold request that enhanced his status eternally. Christian life is a journey of genuine encounters and confession with Jesus. It enhances the status of the confessor before God and contributes to new life in society. The genuine confession of sins has personal and social implications. It builds up a new community that reflects the Kingdom of God in this world.

Jesus: Ideal of Responsible Life

"Dear woman, here is your son…" "Here is your mother…" (John 19:26-27)

On the cross, Jesus could not see all his disciples and the people who followed him during his ministry. But he saw his mother, mother's sister and Mary of Magdalene and one of his disciples (John) whom he loved near the cross. He said to his mother pointing his disciple, "Dear woman, here is your son…" and to the disciple "Here is your mother…" Jesus understood the pain and anxiety of his mother who was grieving for the impending loss of her son. He did not leave her alone but put her into the safe and caring hands of his trusted disciple. In this act, Jesus became an ideal of responsible life.

A Responsible Person

Jesus was born and brought up in a Jewish family which adhered to and followed the Ten Commandments. One of the commandments is 'Honor your father and mother.' Therefore, he knew what his responsibility towards his parents was, especially to his mother at the crucial point of his life and mission. He did not forget his familial duty even though he had gone through the unbearable pain, probably the first time, in his body. It is quite normal for human beings to overlook their responsibilities at the time of the battle of life and death. He always lived as a responsible person to his family and mission. The third statement of Jesus on the cross also shows that he is concerned not only for otherworldly life but also for this worldly life. He lived for a cause that demanded his time, energy and life. But his mother also deserved his love and care even though he came to this world to fulfill a different purpose. The beauty of Jesus' life is that while fulfilling the eternal responsibility Jesus also accomplished his family responsibility. When he realized that he could not take care of his mother, he did not send her to an 'old-age home' (today's language) but into a home where she would live with her 'new son.'

We live in a society where people often behave with their parents irresponsibly at home. For many, old parents have become a burden/obstacle in their career, family life and status. Some tend to ignore their familial responsibilities in the name of ideological and religious commitment. Many old parents live a life of humiliation at the hands of their children. Old age homes are mushrooming in our society. In this scenario, Jesus comes to us as an ideal of the responsible person to the parents. He reminds us that caring for parents needs to be part of spirituality and mission. Human responsibilities at various levels should be balanced. Sonship/daughtership comes with responsibility. In Jesus, we see the embodiment of this principle both to his earthly mother and heavenly father.

New Relationship beyond Biological Bond

By showing his mother to his disciple Jesus said, 'this is your mother' and to his mother 'this is your son. The link between Jesus' mother and his disciple was Jesus. On the cross, Jesus opened a new chapter in human history: building up a new relationship beyond biological bonds. In this relationship, a young man accepted a woman as his mother and she, in turn, embraced him as her son. Jesus' mother became the mother to her son's disciple. Jesus' mother and his disciple defined a new relationship that is possible with human beings. They taught us that Motherhood and Sonship/Daughtership can be defined beyond the biological process. Though Jesus initiated this relationship, they continued it because of their shared faith and mutual love. In his ministry, Jesus formed a new community beyond biological relationships. The early Christian community celebrated the relationships (biblically shaped) beyond biological bonds. Christian faith communities have come into existence through the sisterhood, brotherhood, fatherhood and motherhood developed in mutual love and faith in Jesus.

On the cross, Jesus also redefined the relationship between God and human beings. Sinful human beings became sons and daughters of God. In the context of defining relationships based on caste, clan and ethnicity, Jesus provokes us to build up a community that goes beyond biological relationships. To call someone outside of family, caste, ethnicity as mother or son/daughter needs boldness in spirituality. Only bold people can embrace a biological stranger and get united with him/her in faith to experience the warmth of motherhood/fatherhood. Accountability accompanies relationships. In the Christian community, everyone is accountable for one another irrespective of his/her position, status, birth etc., because this community finds its roots in Jesus who showed a new relationship beyond biological bond. One needs to immerse in the life of Christ to empower himself/herself to say that 'she is my mother/sister/daughter; he is father/brother/son.'

New Journey Begins with New Family of Faith

Mary became a hopeless and helpless person when she saw her son on the cross. While being vulnerable to do anything for her son, she must have stood near the cross worrying about her life also. At that moment Jesus introduced his disciple as his mother's son. Jesus was confident that his disciple would take care of his mother. According to the Gospel of John, the disciple took her into his home. We can infer that Mary began a new journey with a new family of faith. It started from the cross of Jesus. For his disciple also, it was a new journey with new responsibility. The journey began with pain and hope. Had she not been convinced of Jesus' advice to go with the disciple, Mary would not have gone with the beloved disciple. The mother, who lost her son, found hope in the caring gesture (taking her into his home) of the disciple. When Jesus' death threw her into emotional, social (familial) and probably spiritual grief the disciple boldly came forward to uphold her by providing the shelter of a new family of faith. Though there is no replacement for the loss of a son, the faith community/the family of faith can facilitate the life journey of a mother/a father without extremely sensing the loss.

Jesus speaks to his followers as the ideal of responsible life. He tells them to be responsible to the family and build up relationships beyond biological bond and become a beacon of hope to the vulnerable. The Christian community should walk in the footprints of Jesus to embrace the victims who lost their loved ones because of communal violence, natural calamities, oppressive behaviour of the ruling class and social/racial prejudices. On the cross, Jesus told the disciple to take care of his mother. The disciple obeyed him. The same voice echoes even today into the ears of his disciples to take care of the people who suffer from the loss of their children or parents.

Jesus: Model of Relationship

"My God, my God why have you forsaken me?" (Matthew 27:46)

The fourth statement of Jesus on the cross was a question that expressed his experience of pain and forsakenness. People who heard his cry understood the question differently and responded to it differently. Some said Jesus was calling Elijah. One of the bystanders gave him wine vinegar to drink. Then others said, "Now leave him alone. Let's see if Elijah comes to save him." Some might have empathized with his pain and cry though they were unable to help him. Jesus asked this question when he felt that his father completely abandoned him at the crucial point of his life. The Psalmist asked this question before Jesus (Psalm 22:1). Perhaps, before the Psalmist, many would have asked the same question when they had gone through the valley of pain. This question continues with many even today. Questions emerge not only out of curiosity but also out of painful experiences.

A Question of Relationship

The Gospels inform an intimate relationship between Jesus and God the Father. (e.g., John 14: 6f). The question, "My God, my God why have you forsaken me?" expresses the relationship Jesus maintained with God till the end of his mission on the earth. In other words, it is not simply a question of pain and forsakenness alone, but a question of relationship, a question that shows the depth of the relationship between God the Father and the Son. Though he cried out a question, he knew where/ whom he should address this question. He asked a question to a person whom he considered a source of refuge and help. Intimate relationships give space for disturbing and out-and-out questions. In this relationship, the questioner enjoys the freedom to ask any question and the questionee does not upset with him/her. If there was an element of forsakenness in the question on the cross, it was a temporary experience.

This question has another dimension. Jesus came to this world to fulfill the mission of God. His cry should be understood in the context where he was not 'helped' by God who sent him to do a mission. Everyone will go through the experience of asking 'why have you forsaken me' when s/he does not get help from one who has commissioned him/her for a specific work. From a human point of view, Jesus might have gone through an experience of abandonment, but in God's point of view, Jesus' experience of abandonment was part of the mission entrusted to him. It was part of the salvation process. We may also go through the experience of abandonment and ask God 'why have you forsaken me?' At that moment, God will tell us that 'this abandonment is not to destroy you, but to take you into another level of your life as happened in the life of Jesus.' Asking the question "My God, my God why have you forsaken me?" is not sinful but an expression of an intimate relationship with God. There is a moral lesson to this question: we need to listen to those who are abandoned in society. They may not directly ask us 'why have you forsaken me?' But each abandonment is a direct question to our faith life.

A Question of Faith

The question has a faith dimension. Though he was going through pain, he did not abandon his faith in God. He asked this question out of his faith that God would deliver him from this painful moment. He had experienced God's protection and empowerment throughout his ministry. God did not abandon him or throw him into the hands of his enemies until the time of crucifixion. God enabled him to answer the questions raised by the Sadducees and Pharisees. God used him to raise the dead.

God revealed Godself through him. He healed the sick with the power of God. He fed the hungry and courageously stood with the margins of his day. He could overcome painful loneliness at Gethsemane and face the betrayal of Judas. He could face the Roman soldiers and their brutality. He got energy to stand before Pilate and face the prosecution. His boldness, compassionate heart, sacrificial life reflected his faith in God who empowered him to face any challenge. Perhaps, Jesus thought that God would help him come out of this situation as happened in the past. The people who experienced God's care earlier naturally may ask this question.

As mentioned earlier, asking questions is not sinful but losing/abandoning faith at the time of crisis is sinful. We can ask questions but should not lose faith during times of trials and temptations. Jesus is the model in this regard. He asked a question but did not insist on it to get the answer. Rather, he submitted to the will of God. He kept his faith even though he was losing the fight in the eyes of the public. Whether God had forsaken him or not could be answered only after resurrection. The resurrection proved that God did not forsake him but rewarded him for his strong faith and honored him to fulfill the task entrusted to him. For God, a temporary emotional outburst or frustration does not determine the future but the unshaken faith at the time of apparent 'forsakenness' determine the resurrection. The immediate situation of 'forsakenness' should be evaluated in light of divine interventions in the past.

A Question of Hope

This question contains the hope of empowerment. Jesus never thought of utter forsakenness until the crucifixion. By now, he must have realized the plan of God in his life and willingly cooperated with it. He cried to God with a question hoping that he might receive energy to bear the pain and fulfill the purpose for which he came to this world. It means he did not cry with regret or a feeling of helplessness but the hope of empowerment. Jesus' question, 'My God My God why have you forsaken me?' expected the intervention of God. Though God might not have answered the question as fast as Jesus or the public expected, God intervened according to the divine schedule and made Jesus the embodiment of hope to humanity. The person who cried with a question of hope became the source of hope. The cross witnessed the transfer of hope from a person to the entire humanity. The crying Jesus challenges the crying humanity not to lose their hope in God in the time of 'forsakenness.'

The question, 'My God My God why have you forsaken me?' did not end with Jesus. It continues to echo even in our society. How do we respond to the cry of people? 'Cry' attracts the attention of God or fellow beings in a time of helplessness. The followers of Jesus should become 'hope' to those who cry with the question of forsakenness. This hope needs to be embodied in actions that will enable people to inherit eternal life. The question of frustration/pain/forsakenness does not disturb our journey with Jesus. It is part of our intimate relationship with Him, the author of faith and the source of hope.

Jesus: Human for Others

"I am thirsty." (John 19:28)

In the Gospel of John, water appears several times in relation to Jesus' ministry. For instance, Jesus turned water into wine in chapter two. According to the story (2: 1-11), it was the first miracle performed by Jesus. Chapter four describes Jesus' dialogue with a Samaritan woman. It portrays Jesus as source of 'living water.' He told Samaritan woman, "Whoever drinks the water I give will never thirst." In chapter seven, Jesus heals a person, who was disabled for 38 years, near the pool at Bethesda. Now the *Logos* of the entire creation, who turned water into wine, who offered living water, says "I am thirsty." The people who knew his miracle at Cana, his dialogue with Samaritan woman would have laughed at him. Jesus' statement has some implications for the faith life.

Physical Limitation of Jesus

Jesus experienced normal human thirst after long hours of suffering, particularly the painful walk of carrying the cross up to Golgotha. Before the crucifixion, the Roman soldiers mentally tortured him and publicly humiliated him. They set a crown of thorns on his head and mocked him. They spat on him and struck his head many times. They had beaten him and asked him to carry his cross. He was completely exhausted (Matthew 27 and John 19). No biblical account informs whether Jesus asked for water or any drink before his crucifixion. Perhaps, he asked for it, but the soldiers did not give him or he did not ask at all. The statement "I am thirsty" expresses the severity of pain he endured on the cross. He could not bear the pain further without asking for water. His statement should be understood in light of doctrinal creeds that affirm the full humanity and full divinity of Jesus. As a human being, he was physically weak due to many hours of torture and loss of energy. Being thirsty and hungry is the basic physical nature of human beings. Jesus did not hide the natural limitations of his humanity. In the process of salvation, he embraced all limitations of the human body. He not only identified with human beings in their natural body weakness and fragility but also displayed his humanity for saving sinful human beings.

Jesus showed authentic humanity to this world. He lived as a real human being till the end of his life. He did not think what others would think if he asked for water. It did not disturb him because he was conscious of his identity as a human being also. Being truly human does not point to the weakness of Jesus. What matters is the way of perception. His cross taught that human life has many limitations. It cannot survive without positively responding to the limitations. No one can hide limitations for a long time. At the same time, expressing a limitation is not a gesture of weakness but a sign of being authentic. We must be realistic in approach, attitude and actions.

Thirst for Others

Jesus' thirst on the cross has a salvific dimension. Jesus could have avoided the cross and suffering. But he submitted his 'human will' to the will of God for the salvation of humanity. Though he was physically thirsty, his real thirst was for the redemption of humanity and the establishment of God's kingdom. In other words, his physical thirst on the cross symbolizes his missional thirst for others. His earthly life and ministry proved it. He came to the stage of asking for water because of his thirst for others: their life, healing, empowerment and salvation. He became human for others. He lived for others, endured pain for others, spent time with others and finally shed his blood for others. His thirst for others gave him the cross. He gave living water to others but received wine vinegar on the cross. His death quenched the spiritual and physical thirst of others. On the cross, Jesus set a perfect example for his disciples to become 'man/woman' for others. S/he should thirst for the salvation of others, both spiritual and physical.

Jesus' life also teaches that mission for others will make real visionaries exhausted. They work hard for the target groups even to the extent of receiving the cross from this world. Though their thirst for others makes them tired they do not regret it because they are aware that every mission demands sacrifice and pain. Every disciple of Jesus is a potential visionary who ought to live for others who live in the periphery of life. The thirst for others should replace the thirst for self-interest: power, possession and position. The thirst for others is the missional language of the cross. It should be decoded in actions. The cross of Jesus ultimately shows the value of others and the risk involved in the process to redeem human life.

How Jesus' Thirst can be satisfied Today?

Jesus came to satisfy the thirsty lives in this world. He offered living water to the people who were spiritually and physically thirsty. Though no one can satisfy the physical thirst of Jesus today, he still hangs on the cross with his thirst for human redemption. The disciples are called to satisfy the thirst of Jesus by practically proclaiming the message of the cross. In other words, they can satisfy Jesus' thirst by responding to the spiritual and social quests of people. Today's world does not understand the thirst of Jesus. It will try to satisfy people's thirst by giving them (as soldiers did) sour wine in the form of immorality, injustice, impurity, idolatry, anger, quarrel, jealousy, factions, drunkenness (Gal 5: 19-21). But the followers of Jesus Christ should satisfy people's thirst by giving them sweet wine in the form of love, kindness, patience, joy, peace, generosity, faithfulness, gentleness, self-control (Gal 5: 22-23).

There is another aspect to this question. We are the body of Christ. Jesus will be satisfied when we internalize the values of our faith and activate them in this world. Jesus had no regrets for the experience of rejection and thirst because he came to endure it. But he wants us to realize the cost he paid for us.

For that we need to drink waters of love, kindness, patience, joy, generosity and peace from Jesus who is the well of eternal life and quench the thirst of others. When we drink water from this well, we have no other option except to be ready for others, Jesus, the authentic human for others invites us to be thirsty for others, in this world.

Jesus: Successful Completion of Mission

"It is finished." (John 19:30)

When Jesus said, "I am thirsty," they gave him wine vinegar. After receiving the drink he said, "It is finished." What was finished? Jesus came to this world with a divine mission. God sent His only son to redeem sinful humanity. The son faithfully fulfilled it at the cost of his life on the cross. The cross witnessed the culmination of his mission. Jesus finished the work that he started a few years back. Every stage of his ministry reflected the mission of God. His words, actions and journeys revealed the mind of God for the salvation of humanity. At the end, his life became a sacrifice for the sins of this world. His death demonstrates the successful completion of a mission planned in eternity.

Completion of the Divine Mission of Salvation

God's mission through Jesus started with the incarnation of *Logos*. Jesus, the incarnation of *Logos*, proclaimed the world about its sinfulness and the need for repentance and salvation. He introduced himself as the revelation of God and the way of salvation. He was also aware of his mission to the world and participated in every stage of the divine plan without worrying about its consequences. In his missional journey, he encountered temptations and challenges and endured the uttermost pain inflicted upon his body. He took human sin upon himself and fulfilled the requirement of divine justice. For that, he drank the cup of this world that is full of sin. Through his mission, he finished off the power of sin over humanity. He declared to the world that no power could prevent humanity from experiencing salvation. He completed the work of forgiveness between God and Human beings. Thus, he opened a new way to celebrate human life. When his mission demanded his life for the world, then he had no hesitation to give it up for completing his mission.

Every mission envisages successful completion. Its success depends on how the agent responds to the mission. It involves risk and sacrifice. Jesus completed the mission according to the plan of God. The resurrection confirms the success of his mission. He defeated Satan and came out of the tomb. The empty tomb is the sign of the completion of Jesus' mission. Jesus positively responded to the risk involved in the mission. He knew that his death was inevitable to defeat Satan. Therefore, he completely surrendered to the will of God. Moreover, the beauty of Jesus' mission was its voluntary nature. Though God sent him to this world for the salvation of humanity, Jesus voluntarily accepted the mission and laid his life for humanity. Today, Jesus dares his followers positively respond to the mission entrusted to them and attempt to complete it as he did on the cross.

The End of the Power of Law

In the Old Testament, the law refers to the rules and moral injunctions such as the Ten Commandments, laws on rituals and sacrifices, purity-pollution laws etc. The people of Israel gave importance to the law to become righteous before God. They believed that the law would enable them to become righteous. In other words, they depended on the power of law than God, the source of law. Strict adherence to the law defined their religiosity. Though they were zealous for God, according to Paul, they did not know the righteousness that comes from God. For them, the law was the source of righteousness (Romans 10:1-4). They prioritized obedience to the law over faith in God (Leviticus 18:5 and Romans 10:5 f). Instead of becoming the source of the knowledge of God and enabling people to seek righteousness from God, the law became an instrument of power and an oppressive system. At this juncture of human history, Jesus came to give them freedom from the law and righteousness from God. His life and death ended the power of law.

The people who were under the law experienced a new beginning in the ministry of Jesus. For many, the law was burdensome and dehumanizing. The law placed human problems at the periphery. Jesus reinterpreted the law and brought salvation/liberation of human life at the centre of religiosity than the observance of the law. In this sense, Jesus came not to destroy but to fulfill the law (Mt 5:17). He countered the rigidity of law and demanded the custodians of the laws to be compassionate. To the people who considered obedience to the law as the source of righteousness and salvation, Jesus introduced a new law, the law of love. It does not mean that law is insignificant in the process of salvation. The law of love demands faith in Jesus. Faith in Jesus requires a believer to observe the law of God (amended and interpreted by Jesus) in life. The law stipulated sacrifice for human sins. Jesus with his death fulfilled it forever and declared that the power of law came to an end. This also marks the successful completion of his mission.

Work Finished but Continues

The cross and empty tomb witness the mission that Jesus finished for the salvation of humanity. He successfully completed the mission that took him on perilous paths. His mission embraced the unloved folk, the hungry (material and spiritual) multitude, the sinners, the lepers, the disabled, the self-righteous, the unkind rulers, the cruel soldiers and the vulnerable. He encountered the strong to change their attitude and the weak to resist oppression. He challenged the rulers to be kind and the ruled to honor the authority. He experienced rejection, love, betrayal, hatred and finally unbearable physical and emotional pain on the cross. He brought love to humanity, but humanity gave him cross, the heinous punishment of the time. His actions spread the aroma of love and sacrifice. His words brought comfort to the broken hearts and empowerment to the disempowered. His life became a mission! The impact of this mission continues even today.

People who enjoy salvific benefits of his mission, have to continue the finished work of Jesus on the cross. He challenges his disciples to help others enjoy the benefits of this work. We are the ambassadors of his mission in this world. When he says he finished his work, it is implied that Jesus wanted his disciples to receive the baton from him and reach the destination: every human being. Symbolically speaking he prepared the feast; we are called to help others participate in it. For that, we should invite them into the feast of salvation. In other words, he prepared the food of salvation for us. We should eat it every day and serve it to the hungry-spiritually and physically. The cross of Jesus is a call to participate in Divine Mission. A Christian is a person who has already joined the mission of Jesus. S/he must be loyal to that mission till the end.

Jesus: Costly Commitment

"Father into your hands I commit my spirit." (Luke 23:46)

According to the Bible, Jesus uttered seven statements before his death on the cross. In the first statement he declared to the world that he was the embodiment of forgiveness. He assured eternal life to the criminal in the second statement. The third statement shows his responsible life. The fourth statement points to Jesus' intimate relationship with God. Jesus became human for others in the fifth statement. The sixth statement declares the successful completion of his mission. The last statement shows his costly commitment.

The last words of Jesus Christ were the continuation of what he prayed in the Garden of Gethsemane, "My Father, if it is not possible for this cup to be taken away unless I drink it, may your will be done." (Matthew 26: 42). The fulfillment of God's will had taken place on the cross. These words do not contain reluctant surrender but a bold hope of resurrection. He paid the cost for his commitment to God who sent him to this world.

Nonconformity to the World

Jesus in his ministry challenged religious and political leaders of the time for their dehumanizing outlook. He never succumbed to the pressures of worldly powers. The temptation narrative (Matthew 4: 1-11) explains it well. He called Pharisees 'brood of vipers' (Matthew 12: 34) for their negative mindset. He said no to the life-negating systems and practices and affirmed life-affirming values. He challenged oppressive, hierarchical systems of this world and proposed an alternative: the Kingdom of God. Jesus' commitment to God echoed in every encounter he had with the powers of this world. He never compromised his values with the world and its ethos. He called sin by its name. Even the verdict of crucifixion did not affect him. On the cross, he conveyed that none of the worldly punishments could weaken his commitment to God. He knew that he was committing his spirit to the person who was more powerful than the verdict of crucifixion. He could have changed his mind and compromised with the religious and political authorities. The pain could not overrule his commitment. But he endured it and committed to his father for he knew that this pain was worth experiencing to transform the world. Nonconformity is a positive defiance against systemic evil thinking and practices in the world but not the negation of the world.

Today's world (consumerist, competitive and confrontational) directly or indirectly compels people to conform to its ethos. The promotion of subjective truth ignores objective theological and moral truths. The world offers powers to the people who are willing to compromise their faith and ethical values. But Jesus' life and death loudly proclaim that conformity to the worldly systems that are oppressive is sinful. It sows the seeds of compromise in a faith commitment. Nonconformity to the world is challenging, painful and threatening to life. The disciples of Jesus cannot conform to any ideology or system that contradicts the values of the Kingdom of God. Though it is risky, one step of nonconformity in public/community/church/occupation space may contribute to the expansion of God's Kingdom in this world.

Death: The Cost of Commitment

Jesus lived for a right cause, the salvation of people. The powers of this world did not like his words and work because it was empowering and life-giving. His commitment to the cause made him the enemy of the powerful. He propagated the message of love over the rigidity of law. Therefore, he had to live outside the camp. He upheld human life over traditions and systems. He questioned everything that was blind to the broken realities of people. He valued the least over the first. He rejected hypocrisy and embraced honesty. He touched the untouchable and questioned the 'purity' of Pharisaic heart.

He lived out what he preached and taught. His life was the reflection of his commitment to what he believed and whom he represented. He paid the price for what he stood for. The cross was the final location where he finally paid the price for his commitment that saved the entire humanity. Death was the cost of his commitment. However, his death was not the end but the beginning of new life. His death produced millions of people who were willing to die for the cause for which he lived.

Jesus' death gave life to sinful humanity. Today, it invites Jesus' disciples to live and die for the salvation (this-worldly and otherworldly) of others. Jesus tells them that 'stand for others' salvation as I stood for you.' When he calls them to die for others does not necessarily mean that they should die as he died on the cross. It implies the death of human comfort, privilege, ego, and safety for the empowerment of others in society. This form of death may give life to others. The commitment to Jesus results in the salvific empowerment of people. The level of commitment to the poor, the marginalized and the disempowered shows the level of commitment to Jesus and his teachings. Every commitment is pregnant with life.

A Hopeful Surrender

Jesus' words reflect a surrender that is hopeful and rewarding. He did not surrender his life to a worldly power that could make him alive. He knew that this world had no control over his life and tomb. For him, this world can crucify him and inflict pain upon him but not destroy his life. Jesus committed his spirit to God who is the God of Hope. If he had surrendered his life to the world, the world would have anointed him as a ruler or leader. But, there would have been no resurrection. His resurrection was the consequence of his hopeful surrender to the God of Hope. Jesus' resurrection gives hope to this world that the cross breaks the path for resurrection. The cross may be painful, but resurrection gives assurance to the pain. The God of Hope transforms the time of pain into the celebration of victory over the powers that inflicted the pain. Jesus' hopeful surrender teaches that God does not want us to give up at the moment of pain but surrender to him and his ways of resisting evil.

Jesus' last words convey another meaning for Christian life. In a time of pain, God of Hope stands with us and empowers us to surrender to the will of God without losing hope for life. It has spiritual and existential value. God of Hope protects the life in this world and the world to come. The surrender of life to God of Hope also implies the surrender of the human will to God's will, human desire to God's desire and human values to God's values in everyday life.

The seven statements of Jesus on the cross speak to the world that human beings should become embodiment of forgiveness. It will build up a humane society in the world. Every human being deserves to be saved. Therefore, the disciples of Jesus need to work for the salvation/liberation of human beings in respective context. The human communities should be responsible communities where all are cared for according to their needs. The world needs an intimate relationship between God and human beings. It should be reflected in human social relationships. Jesus encourages every human being to stand for others. The disciples of Jesus should participate in the mission of Jesus. Finally, discipleship is a costly commitment.

32

Easter: Celebration of Hope

Christianity stands on the life and work of Jesus Christ. Some events, particularly in the life of Jesus and the early Christian community shaped the faith of Christians. The resurrection of Jesus is one such event that gives historical support to their belief in the resurrection of the dead. Resurrection is the foundation of the Christian understanding of hope. Christians remember the past event of Jesus' resurrection through rituals and celebrations. Easter is celebrated to commemorate the resurrection of Jesus. It falls on Sunday. It is also called Resurrection Sunday. Christians celebrate Easter by attending worship in the Church, exchanging cakes, hot cross buns, gifts, and decorative eggs, and preparing special meals, etc. Easter is not simply a festive occasion of merrymaking or get-togethers. It is a celebration of hope because Easter conveys a message of hope. Easter is the faith declaration of Christians, based on the resurrection of Jesus recorded in the Bible (Matthew 28: 1-10; Mark 16: 1-8; John 20: 1-23 & Luke 24: 1-12). It speaks the language of hope to the people and encourages them to resist the forces of darkness and disempowerment.

Easter as Prophetic Experience

Resurrection symbolizes a prophetic movement. It is the culmination of Jesus' prophetic voice and action. Though His death was the plan of God, His prophetic voice that led Him to the Cross has significance in the celebration of Easter. The political and religious authorities crucified Jesus because He raised the voice of truth. What Jesus upheld was proved true in the event of the resurrection. Therefore, we should celebrate not only the event of resurrection but also his prophetic voice of truth. Remembrance of his courage, vision, and message should be part of the Easter celebration. Resurrection was a prophetic experience because it declared the truth to the world. Jesus said, "I am the way, the truth and the life" (John 14:6). The voice of truth took him to the cross and the empty tomb proved the voice of truth. People killed the truth and buried it because the truth and its advocates disturbed them. The resurrection proved that the truth cannot be killed. The prophetic voice of truth reverberates against injustice, inequality, and oppression even today. It cannot be contained. The resurrection of Jesus was the resurrection of truth. It was a resurrection of prophetic voice and prophetic community. Resurrection strengthened the voice of truth more than ever. It raised many prophets to tell the truth to the power. When we celebrate Easter, we should channelize our prophetic voice. Easter is not simply a festival, but an experience of prophetic voice. It should be celebrated in locations of discrimination and oppression. Easter happens today when the victim says, 'I am free.' Easter celebrations should create more empty tombs in the lives of people. It happens only through a prophetic voice against falsehood, prejudices, and hegemonic mind and oppressive systems.

Easter as an Empowering Experience

After the crucifixion of Jesus, his disciples locked themselves in a room because of the fear of Jews. Jesus' death virtually left them powerless. On the one hand, they lost their Master who taught them and guided them in times of crises; their claims on Jesus shattered on the other. Now, they were afraid to face the world without Jesus. In fact, they faced an existential crisis in their lives. The vacuum Jesus created in their lives was huge that there was no alternative to substitute Jesus. They had neither political protection nor popular support at this point of crisis. They could not expect any help from the religious authorities and the ruling class because Jesus primarily challenged the powerful in society. The disciples became the common enemy in society. At this crucial moment, they heard the good news of the resurrection. For them, it was an experience of empowerment. It was a moment of empowering the powerless. Jesus' visit to their room further gave them the courage to face the world. Though the disciples were initially frightened, Jesus' resurrection gave them the power to stand before the powerful and tell the truth. They boldly proclaimed the Gospel even at the cost of their lives. This is the power of resurrection manifested in their lives. The disciples carried the message of the resurrection to different parts of the world and led many into the experience of resurrection from the bondage of sin. If the resurrection was an experience of empowerment for the disciples, then Easter must remind the people about the story of being empowered in a disempowered situation. Easter should be a celebration of empowering the powerless in society. It invites us to engage with the vulnerable, the poor, and the disadvantaged as Jesus embraced them and gave them life.

Easter: Celebration of Hope

The crucifixion of Jesus shattered the hope of his disciples. Indeed, they were pushed into a state of hopelessness. Though they knew Jesus' declaration that "I am the resurrection and the Life" (John 11: 25), considering the hostile situation, they might not have been in a position to believe that Jesus would resurrect. However, Jesus' resurrection gave them hope to move forward with their mission. It also assured them of eternal life. This hope inspired them to proclaim the Gospel to the multitude and strengthened them to endure persecution. Jesus went through different kinds of suffering till his death on the cross. But his resurrection shows that there is an end to every suffering. God stands with the suffering people. Jesus' resurrection gives hope to those who suffer because of their social status, identity, and faith. The life and ministry of Jesus also inform us that he lived a life of hope. On the one hand, he was always hopeful; on the other hand, others found hope in him. When he was at Gethsemane or on the Cross, though it was a painful experience, he remained hopeful that God would not forsake him. His ministry among the people was an act of hope. When he healed people, he was bringing them back to life and placed them in a sphere of hope. By embracing the social outcasts, Jesus gave them hope for a dignified life. When he challenged the powerful, he was giving hope to the powerless. He taught the lessons of faith and life that imparted hope to people. For instance, his love commandment gives hope to the unloved in society. Hope is the summary of Jesus' life. Therefore, Easter as a commemoration of Jesus' resurrection should be understood and celebrated within the framework of hope. It must be a celebration of hope. Easter should be celebrated through the actions of hope. Actions of hope help people experience resurrection in their lives.